"We are big fans of Halftime. We have been to the Institute and participated in the follow-up coaching. It has helped us tremendously in our personal and professional 'refirement' process. *Trade Up* can help you move from a life of getting to one of giving."

Ken Blanchard, coauthor of *The New One Minute Manager®* and *Lead Like Jesus Revisited*
Margie Blanchard, coauthor of *The One Minute Manager Balances Life and Work*

"Few things in life satisfy me more than watching high functioning women and men use their market skills and experiences to move the purposes of God forward in this world. And very few books clarify the route from here to there. *Trade Up* delivers on that objective. I highly recommend it."

Bill Hybels, founding and senior pastor of Willow Creek Church

"Dean is a natural leader—the next generation of Halftime."

Bob Buford, Halftime founder

"*Trade Up* captivated me from the beginning. As Dean shares his raw and authentic story, he offers a practical, step-by-step guide to finding your calling. *Trade Up* is a must-read."

Diane Paddison, founder of 4word; author of *Work, Love, Pray*

"Dean's story is compelling and challenging, and his message is universal: how to live a life of significance to others—really the only life worth living. And it works. The Halftime message changed my life."

Tomas Brunegård, president of the World Association of Newspapers and News Publishers; former CEO of Stampen Group; chair of Leadership Network of Scandinavia

"If you are a high achiever and success driven, yet feel restless or discontent, then *Trade Up* is for you. Dean shares his deepest self-doubts and personal failings, then how he left the all-too-familiar 'success trap' for a life with meaning and purpose. I've dedicated my second half to this message."

John Sikkema, director of Global Partners; author of *Enriched: Re-defining Wealth*

TRADE UP

HOW TO MOVE FROM JUST MAKING MONEY TO MAKING A DIFFERENCE

DEAN NIEWOLNY

BakerBooks
a division of Baker Publishing Group
Grand Rapids, Michigan

© 2017 by Dean Niewolny

Published by Baker Books
a division of Baker Publishing Group
P.O. Box 6287, Grand Rapids, MI 49516-6287
www.bakerbooks.com

Printed in the United States of America

Library of Congress Cataloging-in-Publication Data is on file at the Library of Congress, Washington, DC.

ISBN 978-0-8010-1958-6

Unless otherwise indicated, Scripture quotations are from the Holy Bible, New International Version®. NIV®. Copyright © 1973, 1978, 1984, 2011 by Biblica, Inc.™ Used by permission of Zondervan. All rights reserved worldwide. www.zondervan.com

Scripture quotations labeled KJV are from the King James Version of the Bible.

Scripture quotations labeled MEV are from The Holy Bible, Modern English Version. Copyright © 2014 by Military Bible Association. Published and distributed by Charisma House. All rights reserved.

Scripture quotations labeled MSG are from THE MESSAGE. Copyright © by Eugene H. Peterson 1993, 1994, 1995, 1996, 2000, 2001, 2002. Used by permission of NavPress. All rights reserved. Represented by Tyndale House Publishers, Inc.

Some names and details have been changed to protect the privacy of the individuals involved.

The author is represented by the literary agency of Wolgemuth & Associates, Inc.

17 18 19 20 21 22 23   7 6 5 4 3 2 1

In keeping with biblical principles of creation stewardship, Baker Publishing Group advocates the responsible use of our natural resources. As a member of the Green Press Initiative, our company uses recycled paper when possible. The text paper of this book is composed in part of post-consumer waste.

green
press
INITIATIVE

For Lisa, Kennedy, and Caden Niewolny.
And for Bob Buford, whose halftime changed his times.

The question is not what we intended ourselves to be, but what He intended us to be when He made us.

—C. S. Lewis

Contents

Part 3 The Destination

Foreword

In 1996, I wrote about my journey from success to significance in a little book called *Halftime*. I crossed my fingers, and book sales limped out of the starting gate. And then they picked up by the box-load. People were saying, "My friends need this too."

Twenty years later, this slender volume from my friend Dean Niewolny, Halftime CEO, confirms that Halftime is no longer just one person's story. In one important sense, it's a significance-to-succession tale. Dean is a natural leader; oficially, he takes the torch now. But you take it, too. The first journey may have been mine, but the next one is wide open. And there's more to know.

If you're ready for the work you were made to do, this book is for you. As you start it, let me tell you from my own experience why your second half, at whatever point in life it begins, stands to beat everything you've done so far.

1. You're more focused now, less likely to drift off course. If you can picture your needs in life as four concentric circles, the circle furthest out is your need to make money and spend it. One circle in is accomplishments, your need to achieve. Next in are your relational needs, met by spouse, children, and close family or friends. The inner circle holds your transcendent needs, what Jesus referred to as "bread of life" and "living water." In the past you may have camped mainly in the two outer circles, but what's ahead invites you to new balance, a keener sense of what falls to the outer circles and what holds your center.

2. You're ready to live out your own agenda. In life's first half, you get a job and put to work the skills that, in most cases, you paid to learn in college. It's true you must make a living, but too often it's someone else's idea of a living. Between duty (which is real) and desire (no less real), a still small voice says, "Is this all there is?" The answer is no, there's more. And you can get to it.

3. You'll gain control of your life. If you're already in your second half, you know the pleasure of that two-letter word *no*. In the past it may have been difficult because you were less sure where to stake your firmest *yes*. All your options looked good, and were good, but not all of them deserved all of you. To know your mainspring and to fix your energies on your capital-M Mission—that's gaining control.

4. You have many resources now. As the decades progress, most of us build up reserves, and not just monetarily. Our knowledge base grows wide and deep. We build a network, and it can hum. We figure out when we're working harder versus working smarter. If life is a car, by our second half we gain speed, traction, fuel, and handling. Some days we're struck by how all those features perform in concert, and this period in our lives can be wildly effective.

5. Demographically, there's more for you. Whatever happened to old age? Our grandparents retired at sixty-five, and their seventies featured orthopedic shoes and hot water bottles. My parents' generation—the Greatest Generation—slowed down for retirement. The good news/bad news now is that a typical "retiree" is still hale and hearty, and can reasonably anticipate another thirty years, most of them in good health with an active mind and the means to grow and go and serve. If you've ever ruminated on what you would do if you were just starting out again, now's the time to bring that out.

6. By now you know you can play through the pain. Hurtful events—an unkindness, or a setback that in your past might have staggered you—have lost their knockout punch. Mentally and spiritually, you're tougher. The NFL keeps a statistic known as YAC—yards after contact, or how far a running back covers after he's hit. Something we know now that we didn't know in our twenties is that we can take a hit and keep pushing. That's a tremendous comfort and asset.

7. Grace fills the gaps. In our twenties and thirties we work to prove ourselves. By our forties and fifties, with competencies piling up, we're less fearful of what we can't do. That's a grace. And here's a question: On a scale of 1–100, with 100 being perfection, where would you place yourself? Where would you place an axe murderer? A saint? All right, say you rank Billy Graham and the Pope at 90–95 and the axe murderer at 8 or 10. (He's bound to have picked up some litter sometime.) You yourself fall somewhere between those two extremes. Yet each person on that scale receives the same gift known as grace. As the New Testament explains it, between you and whatever it takes to rank 100, grace fills the measure.

The past is prelude. What came before is the wind in your sails for what can come next. From the other shore of that great journey: cheers.

Bob Buford

How Did You Do It?

Most often the question comes after I give a talk. Offstage, away from a microphone, inevitably one or two people take me aside and say, "How did you do it? How did you leave the money? The power lane? The stuff?"

My answer is this book.

Whoever you are, wherever you are in life, if success begins to ring hollow and making a difference begins to trump thoughts of more years making more money—if you have a sense of smoldering discontent—you'll like this answer. Whether you stay in your work or enter a new field, when you learn what you're made to do, everything changes.

There's more than here, more than now—more than career, things, retirement, death. You belong to something far bigger than you, and you have a place in a great plan. To the "How did you do it?" question, the answer is: When you're ready for the real goods, you'll be surprised what you can do.

PART 1

MY JOURNEY

The lesson to be learned . . . is the virtue and the advantage and the enlargement of life that comes with having high purpose. That focuses your life. That's what makes you want to get out of bed in the morning and get back to work.

—David McCullough,
in an interview with Ken Burns

1

Is There Not a Cause?

Once upon a real time, long ago in a place still on the maps, on opposite sides of a steep valley, two armies camped in a face-off. On the far hill were the Philistines. On this hill, the Israelites. The Philistines had the advantage, physical and psychological, in a soldier nine feet tall, a freak of nature in custom armor. He packed weapons built to scale. A second man carried his shield.

For forty days, every day, the two armies left their tents in the mornings to line up and face each other across the valley. And every day, for forty days, the Philistines' one-man terrorist cell stepped forward to ridicule the Israelites.

"Send your best man over to fight me!" he'd shout. "Winner takes all!" One hill away the Israelites, led by King Saul, shook in their sandals. (By the way, some sources say Saul probably was the tallest man in Israel.)

One Israelite not at the battle was an old man named Jesse. If you follow Jesus's family tree, you know Jesse hailed from

Bethlehem, in Judah. Of his eight sons, the three oldest were in the army. His youngest was a teenager named David, in charge of the sheep. On Day 40 of "The Israelites Held Hostage" by this face-off, Jesse pulled David from pasture duty to take food to his brothers and their commander.

Jesse's youngest boy arrived at the camp in time to take in his older brothers' daily disgrace. Picture two armies eyeing each other across the divide, again. From the line, Goliath steps forward *again*. He shouts for a taker, again. More humiliation for Israel. Coming onto the scene, David takes in the Israelite soldiers jostling each other in awkward retreat.

Some time before this God had appointed David, through Samuel, to become king of Israel. The appointment was good, but from shepherding to throne room is no single bound. Saul was still king. David still spent his days on the job he knew, in the hills with sheep. Inside David, however, things were stirring. Hearing Goliath's dare, he thought less of his enemy's size than of the offense against Yahweh.

David said, "Who is this uncircumcised Philistine that he should defy the army of God?"

For the fortieth day in the Israelites' serial debacle, the soldiers had no answer. The question, clearly, was rhetorical. In twenty-first-century terms, Israel's soldiers were stressed.

David didn't know when to stop. He asked more questions, annoying his brother. Anyone with siblings knows what came next.

Jesse's oldest son, Eliab, effectively said, "You little troublemaker! Who's watching the sheep?" And David, feeling the put-down, said, "What? You're saying nothing's at stake here?"

That's a modern translation. In the beautiful, evocative, King James Version, David says, "**What have I now done? Is there not a cause?**"

Hear that question: *Is there not a cause?*

Hey, David, why not ask to see the battle plan? Or a vision or mission statement? Or the short-term success strategy? (I have my doubts about their having a five-year plan.) David's question simply pierces to the heart of everything: "**Is there not a cause?**"

As it happens, the question *is* rhetorical. David knows the cause. He's fixed on it. It's about to take him to his sweet spot, the thing God made him to do.

No, I take that back. David doesn't go *right* into what he's made to do. Almost no one does. David is still in God's process. First the young man surveys the scene and frames it in his own terms. He says: "I take care of my father's sheep and goats. When a lion or a bear comes to steal a lamb from the flock, I go after it with a club and rescue the lamb from its mouth. If the animal turns on me, I catch it by the jaw and club it to death. I've done this to both lions and bears, and I'll do it to this pagan Philistine, too, for he has defied the armies of the living God!"

Hold on to the question: *Is there not a cause?*

By now Saul is in. "Use my armor," he says to David. "The king's armor!" And David puts it on. But it's unfamiliar. Too heavy. Too clumsy.

David's back to his own tools, to the way God made him. He loses the armor and scans the area. From a nearby stream, he picks up five smooth stones and drops them in his shepherd's bag. Before a watching crowd of Israelite soldiers, including his three older brothers, David starts across the valley. Read

1 Samuel 17: two armies on the hills and, in the valley between, a mountain of a warrior about to face down a teenager.

Goliath sees "a ruddy-faced" boy, the Bible says. He spits out curses. He saber-rattles. He gestures with sword and spear and javelin. David, I'm pretty certain, is scared but thinking more about God than Goliath. Also, he's skilled at what he's about to do.

For all I know, Goliath is silhouetted against the sun. David tilts his head skyward and says, "Today the Lord will conquer you. And I will kill you and cut off your head." You gotta like that. Victory is God's; the battle is David's.

Then a teenager using all that life so far had made of him, and armed with purpose (and with a laser-accurate slingshot and five stones), face-plants a supersized soldier. The mighty Goliath thuds into rocks and dirt. Grabbing a sword, the teenager removes the giant's head.

Here's another story:

In a Chicago skyscraper, in a fortieth-floor office, a man at a large polished desk stares through plate-glass windows at Lake Michigan. He's thinking that he's worked all his adult life to get to this address or one like it. In the past he felt good about the title, the work, the status, the perks. Now the hole in him dwarfs all that.

After years of promotions, memberships, and big toys, after years of exclusive seating and private access; the latest business books and first-class flights; lunches and dinners and right people in top addresses; hard workouts, costly clothes, power haircuts . . . *after decades on the up escalator* . . .the man is thinking: *If I died today, so what?* And the man is me. And if you'd asked me then, in 2005, "Is there a cause?" you would have gotten the blank stare I most often aimed at Lake Michigan.

At that time I had no mental category for "cause." My ledger headings were achievement, good times, possessions, money, appearances. Aren't life skills for personal gain? But personal gain, for me, was falling short of personal fulfillment.

I saw no giant. I had no cause.

My wife and I were Christians. As our faith deepened, we'd begun to question our priorities, and our appetite for *stuff* was waning. By 2007 we had downsized from multiple homes to one. (This feels ridiculous to say now.) I had made a church mission trip to Africa, where headline words like *poverty, hunger,* and *AIDS* fade into individual faces, real pain, great need. That same year, in November, my wife, Lisa, took a similar trip.

You know the flywheel effect? Jim Collins talks about it in his book *Good to Great*. The flywheel is the part of an engine that spurs momentum. At first you move it, but at some point internal changes acquire their own energy. By spring 2008, my spiritual flywheel had kicked in.

One evening Lisa and I had friends over to show them the Africa project and to talk about the need. Remembering the scene can still make me wince. In our magazine-spread living room, we set out pictures of little faces and bloated stomachs and protruding ribs. Pictures showed young Africans with stumps for limbs and flies buzzing around crusty noses.

You might say Lisa and I were still with the Israelites. Still standing in the crowd of soldiers. We were asking questions. We had viewed the giant. Maybe we hoped the king's armor would fit and we could limit our exposure.

But in our minds the question was forming: Is there not a cause?

That night after everyone left, Lisa and I prayed together. Nothing elaborate. We told God we thought we could use our resources to start an orphanage in Africa. We said he'd need to help us sell our home.

In thirty days we closed on our home in a cash transaction. In 2010 the orphanage opened for operation, and that year we closed out my financial work. That year I also stepped in as managing director of Halftime.

How easy was the transition? Though I felt strongly that it was right to do, I was scared, and I did it in faith, not assurance. As it happens, the word "assurance" rarely shows up in God's lexicon.

There's a story about Mother Teresa. A man asked her to pray for him. And she asked him what he wanted her to pray. He said, "Ask God to give me clarity." Mother Teresa said no, she couldn't pray for that. She said, "I never had clarity; I only had faith."

It's not as if David didn't seek clarity. He asked questions. He assessed. He took in the landscape and listened to people around him. He tried on standard protection, standard weapons. He knew his own skills to capitalize on them. And that all plays in.

In God's hands, however, David's win would not be standard issue. In God's plan for him, David was most himself. Interesting, isn't it? God's victory didn't require another giant or a better weapon. It required exactly David. David: meet your sweet spot.

———— ◆ ————

As you begin this book, I give you three questions.

1. Is there not a cause?
2. In you, is there a sweet spot?
3. What is your giant, and how can you know?

You just read two short stories. In the first, a boy from the pastures, armed with a cause, pushes through his fear. In the second, a man in a tower has no cause. In the first, a boy knows his calling and knows himself. In the second, a man is confused on both fronts.

In Ephesians 2:10, Paul says, "We are God's handiwork, created in Christ Jesus to do good works, which God prepared in advance for us to do." Remember that verse. In it Paul (writing from a prison, by the way) says we *are* born to be part of something big. But *what*? And how can we know?

That's the purpose of this book.

One starting place to know is the Gospels. Matthew, Mark, Luke, and John tell what moved Jesus: his "giants," you might say, of sickness, poverty, injustice, lack of mercy, hunger and thirst, imprisonment, alienation, suffering. The Gospels also reveal that Jesus identifies personally with sufferers: "Inasmuch as you do it to the least of these—*my brothers and sisters*," he said, "you do it to me" (Matt. 25:40, paraphrase).

Question 1: Is there not a cause?
As we attach ourselves to Jesus Christ, our hearts increasingly hurt with him.

I know of a woman abused as a child. As an adult she leads recovery classes for other victims. Once she wrote a haunting paragraph aimed at the adults in her childhood. "When I came to school with a bald spot the size of a silver dollar from pulling my hair, why did you say nothing? When you saw my brother and me leave for vacation with a middle-aged bachelor, why did no one intervene?"

How many people—young, old, in-between—suffer on for lack of someone to see and interrupt?

I think of that when I see men like Dale Dawson step into the lives of Rwandan students. For years the country's best and brightest high school grads had no bridge to higher education. Meanwhile Dale worked at a prestigious financial firm. There came a day when he stepped toward his giant because he had a cause. Now he helps Rwanda's young achievers go to top schools and then replant back home to serve in Rwanda.

In David's parlance, Dale knew how to fight for his sheep against bears and lions. Now he uses those skills to protect God's lambs. But how did Dale know to do that? And of all the causes out there, how does a person know what to do? That brings us to question number two.

Question 2: Is there, in you, a sweet spot?
Answer: Yes, there is. Made by God, remade in Christ Jesus, every person is pre-wired to count in his kingdom, which is no small privilege. You were made with purpose. Even if you messed up on purpose, in Christ you are forgiven, new, restored. Everything that has happened to you, good or bad, screw-ups, rejections, dead ends, and triumphs—*all things*—can contribute to what God prepared in advance for you.

Trust that restoring love. God's passion for you makes it safe to look at your worst—pride, selfishness, what causes you shame and regrets, misfires—and use it to be your best.

Know yourself. As you see yourself (self-examination can take many forms), know your weaknesses and strengths. Both will guide you.

Lean into the way God made you. In tests, conversations, feedback, contemplation (what this book is about), your sweet spot will emerge. You can start to answer questions such as:

When I lose all track of time, what am I doing?

How do I problem-solve?

What does feedback tell me?

In what situations do I thrive?

Halftime helps people find and know their sweet spots—their Ephesians 2:10 calling. Halftimers are women and men who, feeling lost in the their schedules and busyness, begin to carve out the personal space to search and know their strengths, gifts, and passions; to know and be known by others and by God; and to find what they were made to do. Socrates said the unexamined life is not worth living. I meet people who, in an entire life, never come close to a self-exam.

By no means does God's purpose for you mean leaving your job. Mike Ullman, CEO of JCPenney, was called to serve people as he rebuilt a company. Scott Boyer stayed in pharmaceuticals, building a business to help fund essential medicines to the rest of the world. Whether your current work becomes your mission or you move into one, the joy is in knowing God made you for it.

You have a sweet spot. You have a giant too.

Question 3: What is your giant, and how can you know?
At first it may feel as if your giant is your disappointment, depression, boredom, restlessness—your smoldering discontent with life right now. That feeling is not your giant. It's your large nudge.

The nudge says you're ready to know yourself, your loves, your priorities and values and beliefs, and what moves you. Ready to take safe risks. Ready—as God's light reveals you to yourself—to find and take on your giant.

If you choose to look into yourself to find your giant, remember:

You're not the first. Others have made this journey. In their stories you'll see pieces of yourself.

You're not alone. If your smoldering discontent leads you to put significance over success, you have company. Not just boomers or middle-aged mavens, either, but adults of every age.

Insight is not instant. Saul of Tarsus had one blinding vision on the road to Damascus, followed by what some say was up to fourteen years of study. Only then, as the apostle Paul, did he begin to change the world. I doubt you need fourteen years to reach new meaning. But the journey to an effective life takes some time.

The better you know God the more easily you can know yourself, and the more clear your Ephesians 2:10 calling will become. I've rarely seen God do any miracle overnight. Love, children, gardens, healing, friendships, buildings, learning, careers, nature—and life-changing insight—all take time.

Don Stephens founded and heads Mercy Ships—a state-of-the-art hospital on water that brings surgery and healing to "the forgotten poor." Don will tell you that his courage to build Mercy Ships came after Mother Teresa asked him three questions. "I don't know what I thought she'd be like," he says, "but she's one of the most direct people I've ever met."

She asked him:

Why were you born?
What is the pain in your life?
What are you doing about it?

Don told the little nun about his autistic son, something he rarely talked about. She told him God uses pain to prepare us. She took him to a center for handicapped people. He says, "I couldn't pull myself away." When he got back to his home, at that time in Switzerland, he contacted a ship's broker and began to go after his dream. His giant.

A lot of events—inside us and outside—bring us to God. As he brings us to ourselves, we find our cause.

"Is there not a cause?" David asked his brothers. If you've ever asked that question, in any form, keep reading.

2

Wausau to Carmel

The Niewolnys of Wausau, Wisconsin, were short on nothing. Mom, Dad, Dawn, Amy, and I lived in a two-story tract house where my bedroom was the wide hallway outside Dawn's room, and our backyard, which ran into the high school sports fields, was a boy's dream. When I got my driver's license, my dates rode in the family Gremlin. Summers were crowded with hay baling, hunting, and swimming with friends.

In that happy blur, from time to time someone would point out, "That guy's loaded." And I'd post a mental note: *Go to college and get rich.*

Competition was in Wausau's drinking water. My cousin Mark Jehn became a punter for the New York Jets on their practice squad. His brother, Bobby, played running back at Mankato State. Another cousin, Ronnie Seymour, pitched in the Seattle Mariners' organization. And for my early fixation on hard work and winning, the gateway drug was Little League.

In Wausau, Wisconsin, a kid serious about baseball is a magnet for mentors, and as a budding pitcher I drew attention. Dad would catch me if I wanted to practice, and my parents get the Golden Splinter Award for the years they put in on school bleachers. Our mailman was our Little League coach. Also, right in our neighborhood, Bill Rich had played in the pros in the '40s and '50s for the House of David team out of Alabama. I'd pedal my green John Deere tractor around the block, and he'd stop what he was doing and say, "Wanna throw? Want me to catch you?"

The only cracks in the good life were in school. I skipped at every opportunity and cheated on an as-needed basis, which was frequent. How many high-level athletic doors swung shut on my low grades hurts now to think about. And how many scouts came for my pitching, checked my academics, and moved on? Enough that when the time for college arrived, I matriculated at the University of Wisconsin, Oshkosh, not a main campus (thanks to my grades), though it was a Division III powerhouse baseball team.

Never underestimate the role of personal interest in the early Dean Niewolny school of reasoning. Athletics, friends, and girls—in that order—justified my coasting on the brains and work of students around me, and the system served me until it didn't, which happened, thank God, in college during my freshman year.

That day I was out near second base chewing tobacco with my buddies when, in a long double take into the dugout, I saw a suited man next to my coach. *That guy could pass for my statistics professor*, I thought. In a beat I heard, "Niewolny, get over here!" and trotted into a two-man tribunal. "Your test is identical to that of the student next to you," my prof said as roots grew out of my soles. Then he said, "I can kick you out of the university system and you'll never get back in and never get a job—or you can retake the test."

Needless to say, I sat for a second exam and, to my shock, got an honest B, and to a guy who believed he was remedial, this was life changing. Another blindside came late that summer in the second game of a doubleheader. Between games my shoulder had cooled off and, when I pitched again, the joint ripped into a textbook torn rotator cuff. Even with cortisone, I couldn't comb my hair without help, and that was it. Game over. Lights out. Between learning to study and the end of my baseball career, life had turned a sharp corner.

Wages and Means

It was 1985, my senior year in college, when Arthur Andersen, now Andersen Consulting, held interviews on campus for majors in management information systems—a popular major I'd chosen because it was a popular major. On a lark I showed up for the Andersen interviews, and in another shock to all who knew me, I was hired to start in Milwaukee at $22,000. Now a wage earner, my first official act was to purchase a 1982 Pontiac Firebird, and the party commenced.

Purchase number two was a townhouse to bring the party home. In the hours I was forced to earn an income, I huddled in a small room with six other Andersen MIS employees performing systems analysis and keyboard input in Cobol (a computer language) for First Wisconsin Bank. To lighten the drudgery by day, I'd plan my evenings. The programmer next to me would shake his head and say, "Dean, I have no idea what you're doing here."

Turns out his opinion ran wide. Arthur Andersen trains its recruits in St. Charles, Illinois, an hour west of Chicago, where my high school buddy Mike Tullis was attending med school. One evening Tullis picked me up. Driving into downtown Chicago, he said, "I gotta tell you, Dean. I'm shocked you have a real job."

A real job, maybe, but the poor fit, inside me, was nearing critical mass. One morning a colleague said in passing, "You should be a salesman," and that afternoon I walked out of Arthur Andersen and into Piper Jaffrey Brokerage. How much thought informed this critical life move? Just the hard data that (a) girls like stockbrokers and (b) in the *Wall Street* movie that had just come out, Michael Douglas and Charlie Sheen looked pretty cool.

I remember crossing the Piper Jaffrey atrium to tell the receptionist I wanted a job, and his handing me an application. Then he gave me several tests, after which he said, "You blew away the tests, but you're young. Go sell used cars and come back in three years."

My response was to head downtown to Milwaukee's largest brokerage firm, this time with a carpeted foyer of marble, glass, and mahogany, and ask for a job there.

The next morning in the Andersen systems analysis room, I announced, "I'm terrible at programming. I'm going to Merrill Lynch." The woman I worked for, no stranger to my disregard, started crying. Two weeks later I was in new offices, exuberant, surrounded by young guys like me, and studying for my Series 7 exams.

Three Hundred Dials a Day

Maybe the best career advice I ever got came early in my work with Merrill Lynch, from Henry Otten, my sales manager. "To succeed, Dean, you make three hundred dials a day," he said. "At the end of the day you hand in your sheet to show me you did it."

"Dials," of course, means cold calls, the lifeblood of young brokers. *Ridiculous*, I thought. But the advice structured me. Do the dials, and in one year 12,000 contacts produce 120 accounts averaging $50,000. Every day I punched the phone pad until 10 p.m., always calling California last. At close I handed in my call sheet.

No challenge was too high, no task too small for me to compete with someone, anyone, in my twenty-foot radius. We were young brokers all starting out, working hard by day, hitting the bars at night, and the next day back for more. On one of those mornings a call came from Pat, the Merrill Lynch branch manager who hired me. He said, "Dean, my lunch is ready downstairs. Pick it up, and on the way back get me a Diet Coke and bring it to my office."

My job description had overlooked fetching sandwiches, but I left the office and ran the errand. As I sat the sack on his desk, he said, "Young man, today you got me my lunch. Someday I'll probably have to get yours."

The rest of that story came twenty-one years later when I was market manager—regional director—over the Chicagoland offices, and our company merged with AG Edwards. What branch manager now reported to me? The very same, now age sixty. My buddies pestered me to send him out for lunch and a Diet Coke, but it was too late: I was growing up. And by now I was a Christian. Pat, meanwhile, enjoyed telling people he'd hired me and given me my work ethic.

Bad Road Conditions as Metaphor

In Milwaukee, I'd been dating a girl who, finally fed up with my unreliability, finished school and moved to Salinas, California.

Six months into my new brokerage career I called her. "Where are you?" I asked. "Merrill Lynch has an office in Carmel. I'm coming out there."

Wisconsin to California is a three-day trip for a Firebird pulling a U-Haul trailer. Negotiating mountain ice, as most people know, requires four-wheel drive, meaning my trip in a rear-wheel drive vehicle was animated with near-death experiences. Not until I was far up in the mountains and in blinding snow did chains come to mind. Cresting a peak, I felt the car and U-Haul tug downward. Here at the base of an even higher peak, I could make out a guardrail on the left side and a wall of stone on the right. Car and trailer were skidding south when the road turned left, with the guardrail coming at me and the cliff just beyond it.

Right then the weight of the trailer pushed up the back of the car, leaving behind all traction and jerking the car to a 90-degree jackknife. Before a rookie driver could say *emergency roadside assistance*, in slow motion the trailer was shoving the car at the guardrail.

I retell this scene because what happened next seems to frame much of my life. Instead of going over the rail, the car bounced off of it, pushing me back onto the road, which I look back on with wonder.

Double Occupancy

Carmel, a world away from Wausau, Wisconsin, sits on a beach just off Highway 1 between Big Sur and Monterey, on a road thick with cars that cost more than most Wausau homes. When I was a kid, wealthy people were the exception. Now the exception was anything else, and I didn't intend to be an exception to that. With a modest bank account and a cheese-head accent—and with a desk, a phone, and a commute from Salinas—I got down to joining the crowd.

Back in Milwaukee, Henry Otten had told us, "Live two years like no one else wants to, and live the rest of your life like no one else can." All day every day I did nothing but cold call rich people in Carmel and Pebble Beach. Do what no one else wants to; never throttle back. Throw enough against the wall and something will stick. Call. Call. Call. Call. Call.

My "X factor" was to blow past the word *no*. These were cold calls to voices on a phone, not people, so I felt no rejection. When I offered a 5 percent CD and rates were 3 to 4 percent, and I got turned down: their loss. (It helped that people around me got their teeth kicked in too.)

Meanwhile, California swallowed me whole, or vice versa. Bareheaded on my motorcycle, I'd tear down the Carmel Valley Road, long hair flying. My mountainside home had come with a hot tub and scenery. I also bought a Porsche 944—cheapest on the market, but to me it was personal branding. Whatever cog had formed in me in childhood—the one that turned on competing and winning—had slipped into high gear.

Broker of the Day

Broker of the Day means that when someone new comes in to invest, the lead defaults to you. I was that guy one day when a man walked through the door, straight to my manager, Dave, and said, "Don't gimme some whippersnapper. I want someone with gray hair."

Dave popped his head into my office. "A guy here doesn't want you because you're brand new. He wants a gray hair who knows what he's doing."

"Who's the guy?" I said.

CEO of Singer Manufacturing, new to Pebble Beach, he said, here in person to move his multi-million-dollar account from Connecticut to Carmel.

"Will he give me one conversation?" I asked.

Dave disappeared and came back. "One. But no young kid."

In the conference room I met Bill Schmied, a distinguished sixty-year-old in a dark suit with a crisp shirt and white collar. He'd kindly agreed to meet, briefly, with a long-haired poster boy for the California lifestyle, in this case one with a nasal Wisconsin accent.

We sat down, and I said, "Bill, why not me?"

He said, "I've been with Merrill Lynch a long time and I take no chances on my portfolio."

"Bill," I said, "I need to build my business, and you're the most important thing in my world. No one else will monitor your account, look after your affairs, or take better care of you. For a thirty-year vet, you're one of many accounts. Someone like me will be all over this all the time."

Bill had come to California from the far side of the universe. He could have called his Connecticut office for a referral, but this transaction had to be eye to eye. And that's how it happened. We wrapped up our meeting, Bill left the office, and an hour later he called Dave to move the Singer account to me. Right after that I picked Dave up off the floor.

3

Marriage, Divorce, and Real Love

My first wife and I met my freshman year in college when her brother was my roommate—the year UW Oshkosh made it to the World Series.

Nine years later, in Carmel, making the relationship official seemed like the next thing to do, and shortly after, so did a move back to Wisconsin. In a blink the Ryder trailer was hitched to the Porsche. Still with Merrill Lynch, I rolled into Wisconsin feeling as if I were printing money: season tickets to Badger games, weekends in the Wisconsin Dells. . . . It was 1992 and I was in my late twenties. Then came a call from Andy Burish, brother of a good friend from Wausau. Would I want to come to Paine Webber? He mentioned a signing bonus of $100,000.

With Merrill Lynch threats flying at my back, I changed offices to Paine Webber in Madison and began to rebuild a portfolio. My new income paid for a bigger home, a boat and ski equipment, and two new cars. After work I'd slalom until 9 p.m. then fall in bed—the next day, rinse and repeat.

Wasn't this the life? Entertaining in ways small and big. Boating. Tubing. The party had limits, of course, as once-small problems in my marriage grew increasingly inconvenient. I'd tell myself I deserved better, and with a self-ethic far exceeding my marriage ethic, I looked for a way out.

A guy locked onto himself can keep hard thinking at a minimum, and one Saturday morning I sat down and said I wanted a divorce. She sat down to absorb the shock; I moved into a friend's house.

Post-divorce, my world remained boating, drinking, and nights out. Then Mike Tullis called and said, "Trish and I are splitting. Can I live with you? We'll put a strobe light in your living room and make it party central."

The year was 1995. *Forrest Gump* was in theaters, Bill Clinton was in the White House, and Mike took over an upstairs bedroom. An Elvis cutout showed up downstairs, and we added a pool table. The living room *was* party central. Friends materialized after work and from there we hit the bars. Tullis and I were sure our bathroom mirrors reflected back to us the most eligible bachelors of them all right in High Point Estates, in a dream-big house with a three-car garage—one storing a boat. It's a small story, I know now.

Mike and I were working hard by day and partying like rock stars by night when a friend at the office, Kim Marshall, asked me to have lunch with someone named Paul Wilson.

In our group Kim was a listener, and a kind one. Consequently, when she said something I tended to listen to her. Paul and I were about the same age, she said, and had things in common.

When I asked what he did, she said he was a pastor. Stop the music. Wasn't I the guy on the boat living the life of Charlie Sheen? I thought for a beat. Maybe I shrugged. Whatever. "Okay, sure," I said, and she set us up at a nearby Chili's.

And I never saw what hit me. When the day came, Paul and I sat down at 11:30 a.m. At 3:30 I looked up and my life was upside down. For starters, the guy didn't judge me. When I talked about my life he got it, and made no moves to fix it. I wasn't seeking, but whatever he'd found had my attention.

Still Catholic, I was living hard and—a miracle to anyone who knew me—still showing up for mass on Sundays. Over lunch that day at Chili's I lobbed a few loaded questions at Paul, but our conversation mostly stayed easy. How God came up I can't recall. Maybe I said, "How can he allow suffering?" Paul was comfortable even with theology he couldn't know. He said, "What if I'm right? What if Jesus is who he says he is? And what if you're wrong and reject him?" Before we headed out he invited me to a service, and if that seemed odd I don't recall that either.

That Sunday I went alone to Highpoint Church and had my hair blown back. At the time I knew only liturgical worship: kneel, stand, pray, follow the priests' cues. This first nondenominational Sunday morning came with drums and electric guitars—more Billy Idol than Billy Graham. When Paul stepped up to preach he was still the guy in the booth at Chili's. The sermon was as if he was talking to me.

A brief digression here. Two quick scenes. The first is when I was in grade school and driving a tractor down a dirt road. That day, with the crystal-clear logic of a twelve-year-old, I leaned back and steered with my feet. *Bam*, I was on the inside wall of a drainage ditch, the tractor aiming straight down.

Plowing machines are designed for land both horizontal and flat. Thus the small tires front and center. In back, each tire is the height of one man and the weight of ten. In that ditch, the laws of physics should have tipped driver and tractor head over back tire, pinning me under several tons of metal. Yet the next moment the John Deere was midroad with yours truly in the seat, sitting up, and the engine off. That's all I know.

The second scene is Easter in eighth grade. On my own that year I went to every service at Saint Anne's, every day, and I can't say why. In the Catholic Church, the Stations of the Cross depict Jesus's crucifixion to lead us through meditation on Christ's final day. The Sacrament—bread and wine from the priest—are taken as Christ's very body and blood. That Easter week, every time the doors opened, an eighth-grade boy known mostly for causing trouble and skipping church needed to walk the Stations and take the Sacrament.

Both of these pictures—the tractor and the Easter week—I now regard as signposts on the road to Christ before I could read, which is to say that my first Sunday visit to Highpoint touched places already in me. I kept showing up, typically after late Saturday nights, and Paul continued to welcome me. One day Tullis came along and we started going together. No lifestyle changes, just liking the music and service and young people.

Chicago

In Madison, Wisconsin, Paine Webber had purchased Kidder Peabody and offered me a management development program, which I took. Then, interestingly, of twenty-two students, I was the sole graduate, qualifying me to run an office in a midsized city. And yet as offers came in, I deflected them. My town was Madison.

Until the day my boss told me he'd just turned down another management position for me to head sales and training in Chicago. *Whoa.* I stepped into his office. Sales *and* training? I said, "Get me the interview."

It was the position, not the city. Chicago to me was gray skies, standstill traffic, dirty snow, and wall-to-wall people— as if no one there ever went home. Still, a chance to be sales manager—to start Chicagoland's new financial-advisor training program—meant I was becoming somebody.

So at thirty-two I said good-bye to Madison and to everything important to me—friends, boat, bars, partying—to move alone to a city I thought I despised. My anesthetic was the office, especially those first weeks, and late one night the office was where Paul found me by phone. "I'll be in Chicago in a few days," he said. "After work on Wednesday meet me at Willow Creek Church."

Where's the Church?

What Apple, Inc., is to world communication, Willow Creek is to the American church. From the Chicago 'burb of Barrington, Illinois, Willow Creek Community Church is where the word "contemporary" met concepts like music, message, language, style, outreach, and operations—overhauling Sunday mornings for generations. Maybe forever.

Bob Buford, who founded both the Halftime Institute, which I now head, and Leadership Network, a web of pastors/ world-changers, can tell you that behind revolutionaries such as Willow Creek's Bill Hybels, Saddleback Church's

Rick Warren—and a handful of the early 1980s' pastor-entrepreneurs—is a management genius named Peter Drucker, the mastermind who reshaped business post–World War II in the United States and Japan . . . But that's another book.[1]

The point is that on a take-no-prisoners Chicago winter day I took the Kennedy Expressway from downtown to outlying Barrington, located the Willow Creek sign, and turned into, best as I could tell, a corporate campus. After finding a parking space, I hustled through the early dark into a large, warm atrium with a coffee bar and a restaurant where young people in couples and clusters stood with mugs or sat at small round tables.

For me, the disconnects were just starting. In Wausau, the gold standard for event sites was the Grand Theater. More to the point, in Wausau churches came with architectural cues—a steeple, a crucifix in the back and maybe over the altar. This Barrington house of worship would swallow four Grand Theaters and showed no hint of a tower or cross.

In a few minutes, at the far end of the atrium, doors swung out and the foyer emptied as the acre of young people flowed into church. It's what I said: church. And on a Wednesday night. Flowing along, Paul and I landed in center seats and I took in my surroundings. Still no pews, no stained glass, no statues, no fragrance or altar boys. In a few minutes, across a vast, empty platform in front of us, two men rolled out a piano before the audience of two to three thousand.

Onto the stage walked a guy named Dieter Zander, three electric guitar players, a drummer, and three singers. The drummer set a tempo, sound burst out like water through a broken levee, and the large room we were in floated a foot off the ground. My pulse pounded to the tempo. Paul flashed his trademark grin and shouted above the music, "This is church!"

That night I discovered a vitamin deficiency I'd never known I had. Singing lyrics from large side screens, I told myself that if everything else fell away—job, friends, whatever—I'd want to be here, doing this, with these people. From that cold Wednesday evening, I began driving the thirty-two miles from downtown to church on Sunday, Wednesday, and sometimes Thursday's repeat of the Wednesday service. Dreading the trip in afternoon rush hour, I'd fly home afterwards on cloud nine, worship music cranked in my car.

Here was community. Here was a God worth knowing. Thoughts about him expanded into every corner of my life, and every day something or someone blew open more perspective. That Easter when I visited my sister in Minnesota, for example, Chris Carter, Minnesota Vikings wide receiver, spoke at a prayer breakfast. I thought, "Man, this guy has everything, yet he's sold out for Jesus."

A few weeks later with my sister's husband at a Promise Keepers event in Minnesota, I saw my cousin Mark Jehn, my idol since I was a kid. Christianity appeared to be more than church-window saints or television preachers. Or wimps. Around me a stadium of men praised exuberantly and prayed sincerely. The speakers talked about life as a Christ follower and the peace he gives. They talked about a personal relationship with the Son of God, which I knew I wanted, and I bowed my head and said so. My last night in Minnesota as I packed to head back to Chicago, my sister gave me a Bible, which became *my* Bible.

I was in. God existed, and I knew it. I knew he loved me, and I wanted to love him back. But how? Imitate Jesus, I reasoned—love the people he loves. Be a pastor. I called to sign up for a Willow Creek outreach program and they offered me the Good Sense project, to counsel people about financial resources. "No way," I said. Too much like a mailman using his day off to go for a walk.

Even then, hearing my *no* crystallized important thinking for me. My faith was diving deep as my career was blasting off, but finance was not my gig. Never had been. It was the money, not the work—and that would fuel internal conflicts for another decade. For now, it made sense to be a Willow Creek lay pastor, a nonprofessional, nonordained counselor.

Meanwhile, in my social life, I'd become Mr. First Half. I'd start evenings with the gang and peel off around 9:30 because few good things happen after 10:00 p.m. I can illustrate that with a brief account of my Chicago baptism by gunpoint—capping an evening at the Hunt Club on Rush Street, where a few cocktails had spent down my cash. That morning at about 1:30, my buddy and I figured we'd stroll home.

We were headed up Dearborn Parkway, two guys in creased slacks and blazers, when a small commotion flared across the street. I noticed a body on the sidewalk and perceived that the assailant now was running our way. Did I mention his gun was aimed at us? Next thing I knew, that gun was at my temple and a nervous stranger was demanding our money.

When he had both our wallets, he spun me around. A metal cylinder pressed the small of my back and a voice said, "Walk away," which I did.

That morning in the wee hours I lost several credit cards and gained two deep impressions about where to put my faith. The first had to do with fitness. At gunpoint, my body mass index could not extend my life or prepare me to die. I also was a control freak, a type A personality—and control that night was irrelevant. Workouts and a work ethic had been points of pride. That morning was a crash course in their limitations.

In general, new insights seemed to be coming in waves. I was learning that a lifetime of living for myself was poor prep for serving others. Every new Willow Creek ministry I tried was a lesson in humanity, the other person's and my own. And in humility. For several months in a downtown Chicago shelter, I helped write résumés for homeless men and women, a front-row seat both to their feelings of shame and to their dignity. A person is not the job, I learned. Later, as a lay pastor helping anyone who came in, I saw something of the breadth of people's struggles and misunderstandings about God.

And, of course, I was seeing my own misunderstandings. All my life I'd figured that higher morals, or better conduct, or some great personal sacrifice would impress God. That holiness-through-hard-work theory disappeared in one Bill Hybels sermon about "doing" and "done." "All our doing can't do enough," he said. "All that counts is what Christ has done. You just accept the gift."

God had my personal life now; I'd handed it over willingly. But as a compulsive doer, how to give him my workdays? Go to seminary? Join a nonprofit? Write big checks? Start an outreach? About that time another Hybels sermon calmed me. "If everyone left the marketplace for the ministry," Bill said on a Sunday morning from downstage, "who would be a light in a dark world?"

I wanted to be a light. That I knew. To up my wattage, in a given week I would take classes, hear about and read books, watch videos, join outreaches and studies, go to concerts, make new friends . . . and my energy for it was telling. Financial courses to advance my career had barely held my interest. Now as opportunities opened to learn about Christ or be at church, I inhaled them. One Sunday morning, it made all the sense in the world for me to be at church with a beautiful young woman named Lisa O'Brien for our first date.

Even courtship was changing. After an extended stretch of few to no dates, a meeting at a restaurant (we'd both come in groups) had led to an hours-long conversation with an amazing young woman. That led to my driving to Joliet, Illinois, through dense traffic, making me hours late for dinner with her parents, sisters, and brother. When I arrived, full of apologies, I was shown to a lone plate of dinner on a table that had otherwise been cleared.

"You didn't think we were going to wait for you?" the O'Briens said, and I was home.

From the start, Lisa was the place I could be myself, and better for it. Yes, she is beautiful. But her kindness and loyalty are in their own league. Lisa and I met in September, got engaged in December, and were married in June. This time not because it was "time," but because it was right.

In the next decade, our family would take shape as our two kids came along: a daughter I can only describe as like Jesus, a son any father would want. And family gave my life great meaning. But how to serve God with my professional skills seemed to stay beyond reach. For years now, I'd stayed at Paine Webber with no sense of fit. Except for the paychecks, my workdays spent helping wealthy people increase their wealth had lost their luster. As Bob Buford so famously pinned it, I'd had enough of success for its own sake. Now I craved significance.

Faith in Financial Services

For the record, I tried hard to make my work my ministry. At UBS, which by now had acquired Paine Webber, I formed a 7:00 a.m. Bible study, which drew seven or eight people and sailed along until a broker complained to my boss that the study would engender favoritism.

Moving the study to a nearby hotel, I strove to serve my associates in the office. Once a day, at least, I'd walk the floor to be open to anyone having a tough time or just needing to vent. Several great talks and relationships surfaced, such as when a Muslim friend challenged me to show him where the Bible says Jesus is God. I found the passages (not hard) and learned so much that I wrote twelve pages about it. Coming off another conversation, a Jewish friend and I read together through Isaiah 53—sacred scripture for both of us, though Christians believe the passage foretells Jesus's crucifixion.

Scores of conversations—too many and often too personal to recount—enriched the hours and my work relationships, and they stay with me. Bill Hybels was right about Christians in the marketplace—in Christ's love, careers can become callings. The work is purified, as someone put it. Instead of money, you're working for a cause bigger than you. Stress drops. Joy trends up. Except for me, it didn't. For the calling inside me, the corporate world with its legalities and compliance issues increasingly felt like handcuffs.

As for the paycheck—my strongest tie to work—more and more the thought came to me, "How much is enough?"

4

The Move to Meaning

One sunny Chicago afternoon on the fortieth floor of the Mercantile Building on South Wacker Drive, I exited Wells Fargo Advisors' offices, took the elevator to the fourth-floor garage, and drove the Kennedy Freeway home, all for the last time.

The decision was hardly overnight, as evident by now. Humans resist change until a seismic event forces our hand, and in my case the earthquake was spiritual. The more I grasped God's love, the more I saw his value on certain things with no price tag. My "smoldering discontent" regarding life as usual had burst through the surface. My exit actually started, I think, in 1999 on the night Bill Hybels interviewed Bob Buford on the Willow Creek stage.

First I'd like to say that the strongest impression from that night is unrelated to Halftime. The most powerful moment came with Bill's tears as he said, "Bob, I worried that after Ross died you would lose your faith, but that didn't happen." Bob and Linda's adored and adventurous only child, twenty-four years old and living in Denver at the time, had died swimming Texas's Rio Grande with two friends. Later in the interview I heard Bob utter his "success to significance" phrase, and that's what charged my thinking. All my life I'd thought only priests or altar boys could be spiritually significant. Bob said service to God comes out of who we are naturally.

At the time, my marketplace mind-set was still to make money and acquire toys. If significance was calling, I flagged it as a wrong number. Helping out at church should be enough. I also worried that what God had for me, if there was more, would involve personal sacrifice. And who wants that?

It was four years since I'd become a Christian, three since I'd heard Bill Hybels say the commercial world needs more believers. Another six or seven would pass before I knew beyond a doubt that I would not be God's gift to the business world. Bob's gift to me that night, in his talk with Bill Hybels, was his saying that how we can serve God far exceeds either "stay in business" or "go to seminary."

Before I could trade high pay for high purpose, though, I had to want something more than I wanted money. I also had to "start with the end in mind," as Bob reminds us, and break down any big, scary potential changes into small exploratory steps. My goal now was "a life of joy, impact, and balance"— hardly a Grade-A mission statement by Halftime standards, but it got me started.

By early 2000 I'd also begun what Halftime calls low-cost probes. Because I cared for the homeless, I worked at a shelter. As lay pastor, meanwhile, I also waded into a broad spectrum of people and problems. At work I pursued ways to minister to my staff and colleagues. And during that time, Willow Creek put me on a satellite church-planting team in Wheaton.

Not one of those things got me out of bed in the mornings. Like many Christians unclear on their callings, I had hoped service was an end in itself. But until we serve from our gifts, I'd learn, the work has scant staying power.

For my part, I kept on seeking change, usually shooting in the dark and occasionally scoring a hit. One week, as the thoughts came to me, I wrote down all my likes and dislikes. By the end of the week the list staring at me said I operated as an extrovert, but I wasn't one. Rather than go wide with people—a cocktail party for fifty, say—I was the guy to spend hours in a living room with four or five friends. Good to know.

Paradoxically, and just as important, I worked best in a team versus on my own. Solitude reenergizes me but I need people. My managerial style was face-to-face, as opposed to virtual or phone meetings. For team reports, I'd want everyone physically together. By 2004 or '05, my search had no formal structure, but the product (me) had definition, if not real direction.

By 2006, alone in my office one day and staring out at Lake Michigan, it all came to a head. I erupted with, "Surely, *surely* life is more than this!" And though they burst out in anger and angst, the words brought me peace. Very clearly the thought came to simplify. Not audibly, but internally, I felt God say, "I have other plans for you."

I said to myself, "Whose economy do I want to be on—the world's or God's?" At this point I saw myself as a success on my economy and failing on his.

Bob Buford

On our first date at Willow Creek, I'd said to Lisa, "So you know, my desire is to leave my work someday and be a pastor."

51

I'd said it with no sense of calling, just restlessness. And that day Lisa had smiled and nodded. A few years later, after hearing Bob Buford at Willow Creek, I told Lisa again, with new resolve, that my future was not in finance, and that it probably was in the church. That time she looked at me and said, "You've said this before."

Now, in 2006, she was on board. She said, "Honey, it's time to explore. I know you're not happy where you are." Soon after, the call came from Keith Vanderbeen, my regional president at Wachovia, inviting me to a book study of *Halftime*, by Bob Buford.

Buford . . . the name had drifted into my mental back files. And the word "halftime," in this context, was new. But a whole book about the search for significance? Keith called the group a "Halftime Huddle," and by any name I was in . . . alongside lawyers, investors, and advertising whizzes.

Brief background: About the time I left college in Oshkosh, Wisconsin, for my first job at Arthur Andersen, down in Texas Bob Buford was the forty-something head of the runaway success known as Buford Television. And he was outgrowing it. "The art of the deal and the thrill of the kill," as he puts it, had begun to bore him. In his youth he'd thought about the ministry. Now facing his life's second half, he wanted more than a bank statement.

Bob was not a saint; he was a business guy. But he wanted to care for the people Jesus cares for, and he prayed and no clouds parted. No figure appeared to lead him out of the world he'd made for himself. So with a mind sharpened in a thousand business challenges and polished by leading a national company, he used his business skills to rise above business as usual.

As I would do many years later in my own DIY halftime journey, Bob started with self-evaluation and set a goal of "significance." To appraise his skills, talents, and interests he applied both standard tests and personal feedback. To pin down his passions, he talked to experts in multiple fields, and I mean top experts. One notoriously savvy consultant Bob commandeered as his personal coach. Bob kept notes, charted his progress, and leaned into hard questions about his faith and priorities. Eventually he opened a path not to a life of check-writing philanthropy but to a new model of taking business skills to human needs.

Bob's mentor, Peter Drucker, advised and applauded as Bob's second half split into two organizations. The first, from a career of networking and gaining best practices, would boost America's evangelical church. Leadership Network would equip Christian leaders with management skills to scale ministry to people's needs. As only he could, Bob brought Peter Drucker to a generation of entrepreneurial young pastors like Bill Hybels and Rick Warren. That national organization of pastors is still thriving.

In the second organization, Bob would help individual marketplace leaders crown workplace success with life significance. Recasting business skills for human service—in for-profits and nonprofits both—became his part two, called the Halftime Institute.

Bob's new bottom line would show up not on ledgers but in lives. As Peter famously observed to him: "The fruit of your labor grows on other people's trees." Bob outlined his journey in a book called *Halftime,* and as I read it in 2006 for my Huddle, the words fell on fertile soil. Before long, between Bob and me, it would be common ground.

In May 2008, three Wachovia colleagues and I trekked to the Halftime Institute in Dallas for its two-day Launch Event. For the first time, I heard Bob say the journey is not just success to significance—but from success to significance to surrender. Bob also drew a picture of Jesus meeting us at our deaths with just two questions: "What did you do about me? And what did you do with the gifts I gave you?"

Question one of that exam I could answer. I'd taken Jesus at his word and, like a man walking onto a frozen lake in winter, I'd put my full weight onto trusting him. The second—what I did with the gifts he'd given me—had brought me to Halftime with two questions of my own: Is it possible to do good and still not be where he wants me? How could I know whether I was aligned with my God-given gifts, talents, and abilities?

I could park cars at church on Sunday mornings, take care of kids, minister to the homeless—all with a full heart. But on God's behalf, did that leave me as a twelve-cylinder guy serving on six cylinders? This wasn't vanity, I hoped, but accountability. How to know?

Halftime coaching was optional then, so I hired Jeff Spadafora, a certified Halftime coach, who said, "If I can't get you figured out in five months, I'm not doing my job." (A year and a half later, still working at it, we laughed about that.) Jeff introduced me to steps I hadn't known to think about. Getting into spiritual and financial health, for instance, and squaring myself first as husband and father. Once secured in the basics, we could focus on, "How has God wired you? And what's he calling you to do?"

Already I resonated with the Halftime mission to help high-capacity leaders get to their Ephesians 2:10 callings. On the screen in my mind, the "rat race" is a street in New York City's financial district, suits scurrying from office to office, meeting to meeting, deal to deal, until the souls inside them implode. I'd think of Jesus's "My burden is easy and my yoke is light." I'd think, "If they knew their Ephesians 2:10 calling, God's sweet spot, they could know joy, balance, impact, peace."

"Jeff," I said once, "I feel as if Halftime, the organization, is my halftime," which he quickly doused with, "No budget for that." Around that time I also interviewed by phone with Tiger Dawson, then Halftime's managing director, wanting to partner Halftime with financial service experts. Neither conversation gained traction. I stayed with Jeff's coaching.

In early 2009, Lisa and I had another long talk. Life had to count more for God, I said, and she agreed it was time. On a cold day in March, driving from Chicago to a branch office in Oak Brook, I said to my boss: "Patricia, I think I want to leave and do something different."

"When everyone else is looking for work?" she said. "You sure?" Over the next six to seven months, she and I built an exit strategy.

By September 2009, at the end of my phasing-out period at work, I let Bill Hybels know I'd pulled the 'chute. One day later a Willow Creek rep called to tell me about opportunities there. Ten years earlier if Bill had asked me to be third-string flower planter on the far back lot I'd have signed. Now the work to understand both myself and God was paying off. As of yet I had no *yes*, but I could give Willow Creek offers an informed *no*.

Weeks later at a dinner in the Hybels home, Bill said, "Dean, tell everyone what you're doing," and I had to say, "I'm still not sure." (Red alert: this violates the Halftime Tarzan Rule to release the current swinging vine only after you've grabbed the next one.) Bill said, "Oh, boy, we better pray for Dean." And they did.

Then, only a month later, two events—a job interview and a Halftime weekend—took Lisa and me to Southern California, where we'd agreed we wanted to live. Night one of the Halftime event, a man I didn't know pulled me out of worship to say, "Four guys here say I should get to know you. May I come to Chicago for a weekend with you?" Worship music was still surging as I returned to Lisa from talking with Tom Wilson, head of the umbrella organization of Leadership Network and Halftime. When the service ended, Lisa said to Tom, "Come see us in the summer when it's warm," to which he said no, it would be next month.

Then, that night in California, in our hotel room, about 3:30 in the morning, Lisa sat upright in bed. In all the world, my wife wished most to live in Chicago or Orange County. Our hunting for property in OC was, I think now, an attempt to be significant for God on our terms. Now she said to me, "I had a dream. That man is coming to our house in Chicago to name you the CEO of Halftime, and we're moving to Dallas."

"Craziest thing I've heard," I said. "I'd screw that place up so fast." (Still to be determined.) "I'm sure they want to talk to me about the financial services industry."

As usual, Lisa was right. Tom showed up and asked me to interview for managing director of Halftime, sending my thoughts back to the conversations with my Halftime coach, Jeff. Only in retrospect do the pixels crowd into a discernable picture. I thought of the head-on-desk, "there's got to be more!" scene in my office, my Wachovia boss forming a Halftime Huddle, and the Halftime Launch. I thought of my passion for helping high-capacity leaders and the job interview in Southern California that folded so easily into the Halftime event.

After an interview series that makes the presidential primaries look simplistic, on February 22, 2010, I was named managing director of the Halftime Institute. I said to Lisa, "You weren't completely right. I'm managing director, and not CEO." A year later we restructured, and I was made CEO.

PART 2

YOUR JOURNEY

Your death will be like the final buzzer at a basketball game. No shots taken thereafter will count. If you've failed to use your money and possessions and time and talent and energies for eternity, then you failed—period.

At your death, the autobiography you've written with the pen of faith and the ink of works will go into eternity unedited, to be seen and read "as is" by angels, the redeemed, and God himself.

With that in mind let's get clear on our life calling so when your final day comes God will be there and say you have finished strongly—well done, my good and faithful servant.

—Randy Alcorn, *In Light of Eternity*

Now to Rewrite Your Own Ending

Don't ask what the world needs. Ask what makes you come alive, and go do it. Because what the world needs is people who have come alive.

Howard Thurman

Trade Up swings 180 degrees now from what I did to what you can do—from the narrative of my life to an invitation to rework the ending to yours.

The next chapters spell out real steps that have been tried and found to work. You know not to expect a day in the park, and by no means can you do it solo. But the sanity you gain, your growing rapport with others, the self-knowledge—the sheer adventure—are worth everything you wager: your time, your picture of yourself, and maybe some profitable pain.

You may end up halfway around the globe. You may open new worlds right where you are. You can't know. What's possible to know is the person you wish to be, which leads to the first chapter in the how-to section of *Trade Up*: "Start with the End in Mind."

5

Start with the End in Mind

It's your eightieth birthday and someone has taken you to your favorite restaurant. Stepping through the front door, you see the entire place has been rented out for the occasion. Across a large room you scan the faces of some two hundred family members, friends, and business associates. You notice a stage and microphone.

After dinner, one by one, all of the guests—your spouse, your children, your neighbors, employees, associates—form a line to take the microphone and say to everyone what your life has meant.

What do you hope to hear?

———— ◆ ————

This question brings to mind a funeral I attended during my years at Wachovia Securities. I was there to support a woman at work, but the deceased person was a stranger to me. Best I could tell, this woman had no wealth, no notoriety, no material possessions to speak of, none of the bragging points that people like me would have sacrificed entire families to gain. I said to a man next to me, "Who died, and why are all these people here?"

She was a teacher, the man said. *And this is her final classroom*, I mused. No five hundred people would show up to mark my passing, that I knew. Of the few who might see me off, any one could step to a podium and pretty easily sum me up: lucrative career, owned a lot of stuff, had a good time, into himself.

By that point I'd been a Christian for several years, and everything about this funeral was a punch in the solar plexus. Most of my life I'd bulked up for society's scales. Now on the measure that counts for everything, here was a real heavyweight. And it wasn't me. I imagined this teacher leaving this life to the words, "Well done, good and faithful servant." If I had been the one on a deathbed, the best I might have hoped for would have been, "Well, Dean, you made some big money and had quite a few things. Good for you."

---◆---

So back to your imaginary birthday party. As you consider the final commentaries on your life from the people who know you, three questions can help you use that picture to improve your life, starting now.

1. What is all your gaining costing you?
2. What in your life is priceless and what are you doing to protect it?
3. If you were to reorder your life to finish well, what evidence would confirm that you were on the right track?

Question 1: What is all your gaining costing you?

At one Halftime Launch Event—the two-day kick-start to a yearlong Halftime journey—a well-known C-suite executive named "Bill" was there. After heading a forty-thousand-employee American company, he'd come to evaluate his life and choices. He was wise to do it in a sympathetic group because his career review came with pain. For decades Bill had given his best to his company, and no question it was thriving. The high cost of what he gave professionally, though, left craters in the home that lay exposed, and in the lives of his kids and former wife. Now he was sixty-five years old, living in an *Architectural Digest*–worthy home, surrounded by thousands of acres of breathtaking mountain scenery, and mostly alone.

Early in my own marriage, the drive toward my ideal net worth had dinged relationships with my wife, Lisa, and with our kids. Lisa is a beautiful woman with head-turning talent around acting, speaking, television, and hosting. Among other things, she cares deeply about single moms and their kids. Seven or eight years ago, with little active support from me, she wrote a book called *Girls of Greatness*, a safety guide through the white waters of young female adolescence. From that book came an entire ministry, now a nonprofit in the United States and the United Kingdom. But I valued her values too little.

Once, for example, Lisa had an opportunity in Chicago to act in participatory theater and I pooh-poohed it. "You'd miss my company Christmas party," I said. "And I'm head of the company." (It's painful now to write that.)

There's more. While Lisa and the kids got by with less of me, the constant stress from my all-important work produced hives on my upper arms and biceps. Ever had hives? Unbelievably painful. The doctor told me that the burning, itching red rash tied directly to my state of mind.

I confess all this to illustrate that the "Bill" of the story who sacrificed his family to his work is hardly exceptional. In my case, all my gaining was costing me my primary relationships and my health.

Once, in the *Washington Post*, I read that Harvard researchers had discovered the one thing everyone needs for happier, healthier lives. Care to guess what that one thing is? Relationships.

Dr. Robert Waldinger, a Harvard psychiatrist, took a seventy-five-year study of a group of men, young adult through old age. He concluded that the happiest and healthiest participants "maintained close, intimate relationships."

Waldinger says lonely people are less happy, their health declines earlier in midlife, their brain functioning declines sooner, and they live shorter lives than people in relationships. Then he added, "And good, close relationships seem to buffer us from the slings and arrows of getting old."[1]

Enough said.

Question 2: What in your life is priceless and what are you doing to protect it?

A man with a notable answer to this question is a Halftime director who, once a week, devotes an entire day to his wife. On that day they take walks, go sailing, see a movie, play tennis. To the rest of us he's unreachable.

Ouch, because, at the spinning Niewolny house, unless I'm deliberate, my time goes to whatever seems urgent. Unless and until my assistant, Jan, marks my calendar with my son's games and my daughter's recitals—and date nights with Lisa—family time takes some hits.

Scheduling events, however, is only part of protecting the priorities in my life. I also repeatedly have to comb through my calendar to remove nonessentials and create white space for (a) time to exhale, and (b) room to respond on short notice. I'm better now at opening white space, but as an achiever, wired to accomplish or do things, unspecified time still feels wrong. I say this even as I regret the years swallowed whole by my compulsions around my career—and even though I know the long-term payoff when I give my hours (including the down hours) to the people who *are* my life.

Question 3: If you were to reorder your life to finish well, what evidence would confirm that you were on the right track? For me, evidence of my finishing well would show first in Lisa. She would know her calling and be in it. Instead of our marriage drifting into coexistence, we'd be more in love, meaning I'd kept our relationship a priority. Our grown kids could confidently take on life for themselves, and they'd walk with God. Lisa and I would give money and other resources to the things Jesus cares about. We'd watch our health. And to the best of my ability, I'd know I was doing what I'm made to do. (Keep in mind, I'm sketching an ideal.)

A raft of research backs me up on saying that life's riches reside in people and purpose. One article I keep on file quotes the Mt. Sinai Health System's statement that a life with purpose actually reduces death.

Wait a minute: "reduces death"? With one notable exception, mortality is 100 percent. But to quote from the Mt. Sinai report: ". . . a high sense of purpose is associated with a 23 percent reduction in death from all causes and a 19 percent reduced risk of heart attack, stroke, or the need for coronary artery bypass."[2] How about that? Purpose keeps us here *longer*.

Dr. Viktor Frankl, a brilliant Jewish psychiatrist, was swept into the Holocaust that scorched through Europe in the 1930s and '40s. Through several years in slave labor and in work or death camps, including Auschwitz, he witnessed firsthand and in the worst conditions what can keep humans alive.

Frankl saw physically strong men give in, curl up like dry leaves, and die. He saw supposedly weaker men, prisoners he'd have judged as doomed, somehow hold on. Other things being equal, the difference was hope: whatever stirred meaning and purpose for that person. Even in extreme conditions, people with a reason to live—a child to care for, a spouse maybe still alive, something required of them—could survive overwhelming odds.

In the camps Dr. Frankl helped prisoners identify their purpose and somehow endure the hell. After the war he poured what he had learned, anonymously at first, into one of the twentieth century's most important books, *Man's Search for Meaning*.

When Jimmy Fallon had an accident and nearly lost his ring finger, during his week off for surgery and recovery he read, of all things, *Man's Search for Meaning*. On his first evening back on TV, America's premiere nighttime talk show host held up the little classic written seventy years ago and said, "The meaning of my life is I belong on TV and I should be talking to people . . . and if anyone's suffering at all, this is my job. I'm here to make you laugh. . . . That's why I'm here."[3]

Wherever you find people—in death camps or on talk shows, or in the 'burbs—you can find the amazing, life-giving power of purpose. Even among those who have been in the workforce for many years, there is often a willingness to change careers to gain greater purpose. We come with a DNA-driven desire, a physical compulsion, to know why we exist and to act on it. And the majority of us, however we define success, come to a time when having it for its own sake pales next to the real trophies of true direction: our effects on other lives, a chance to make a difference.

And it's never too late, or too early, to get it.

6

Open Your Time and Space

Ninety-nine percent of new Halftimers are textbook type A's, men and women shrink-wrapped into their schedules with zero margin. They walk into the Institute grafted to cell phones, setting plans by the quarter hour. When we tell them, almost first thing, to open their calendars and pry open their hours (for whole stretches, ongoing), it's a little like waving scissors at a patient's morphine drip.

For their part, our Halftimers report back to us that their early efforts to dial back on busyness are (1) scary, (2) a relief, (3) welcome, and (4) incredibly hard.

My sympathy goes out to them to a point. Get past the fear, I say. No margin, no mission. The journey out of our comfort zones and into our souls demands time to know ourselves, to know who God is, and, ultimately, to have the freedom to act on both.

Of course, the things that hold us down are seldom bad. It's the old saying that the enemy of the best is the good. But parsing good from best—pastimes from priorities—can be tricky. So at Halftime we reach into our bag of tricks to help, and the chart below is significant help. Do it now and you'll thank me. It's simple to fill out and, when it's complete, like *that* you have a picture of your good vs. best—all you do in light of what you value most.

Your chart will be a longer version of this:

Activity	Heart	Impact	Growth	Obligation	Total

In the far left column list your activities morning to night, week to week, month by month, and through the year. Type A's will know this drill. It's a *list*, remember—not a judgment—so be honest. Scroll through your waking hours from alarm to treadmill to shower, dressing, breakfast, commute, standing meetings and conference calls, sports events, golf dates, lunch, commitments . . . everything. To the right of each activity, under columns headed *Heart, Impact, Growth,* and *Obligation* (all four), rank that activity 1 to 5—low priority to high.

In the rankings, also, brutal honesty is your friend. Something purely optional like making it to Krispy Kreme as the oven doors swing open maybe gets a 1 under *Obligation.* On the other hand, a spouse's event may earn a 5 in both *Heart* and *Obligation.* A professional course, the value of which only you can judge, may get a 2 for *Growth* but a 5 for *Obligation.* Keep at it.

When your list and rankings are complete, at the far right of each activity tally your totals and consider the results. As you peruse your numbers—high and low—ask two questions:

1. What low-value activities can I eliminate?
2. Of the remaining high-value activities, where can I double up?

Until someone convinces me otherwise, *People* magazine, Facebook, Instagram, and most television shows qualify as black holes. As for "doubling up," this is your cue to get creative. The game is to combine activities, like reading a book while on the treadmill or meeting a client for lunch. The point, always, is to open your free time.

Back in Chicago I was taking some first steps to open more daylight in my calendar. A few years before, I'd earned my pilot's license and bought a Beech Bonanza V-Tail. Now there was no avoiding the fact that my love of flying swallowed too many family hours, and flying got grounded. My standing golf dates—by the time I got ready, played eighteen holes, and debriefed at the clubhouse—likewise devoured prime hours for time with my kids. I could tee off other years.

After our family moved to Barrington, Illinois, my train commute allowed time to hit high points in the newspaper and do the Bible course I'd been studying at home. Getting to work early bought me minutes to check through my day there sooner. It also freed up Thursday afternoons for downtown Chicago's Hope Center, where I helped homeless men and women write résumés.

More recently here in Dallas, when a business trip took me to Pepperdine University and my eighteen-year-old daughter was out of school, I had her fly with me to California. After my meeting, she and I cruised Malibu, my old stomping grounds, and looked over Pepperdine.

In my finance industry days I knew that every activity had either to generate revenue or build profit. If I wasn't recruiting new brokers to raise income I was looking for ways to cut expenses. That principle still holds. Unless a phone call, even a cup of coffee, is on Halftime mission, it gets a polite no. It has to. I know why I'm here, and what I learned from a chart like the one in this chapter helps me stay on task.

Back in my days as a young broker trainee in Princeton, New Jersey, $2 million producers (meaning they took home a half million a year) told us they "reacted" only four hours a day. The work to track down a missing dividend check or to ask to have a statement explained got their attention from 8 to 10 a.m. or from 3 to 5 p.m. During prime time—10 a.m. to 2 p.m.—these big producers were proactive, period. All work was outgoing. The inbound calls they accepted sure as heck better relate to a revenue-producing trade.

The years since had taught me that the difference between proactive and reactive is the difference between my agenda and someone else's. Yesterday in my calendar I assigned two "no appointment" days to focus on mission goals, so I don't risk losing those days to reaction. There's a time to respond to incoming things, but it's seldom prime time.

So use the chart to sketch your priorities, and then plan your hours to honor them. You may actually enjoy the exercise.

Margin in My Treasure

As I grew more aware of how I spent my time, I saw that a lot of it went to upkeep.

Lisa and I had built a home in Illinois where we could walk from the house to the hangar, jump in our plane, fly to Wisconsin, and transfer there into our parked SUV. Then we'd drive to the lake house, amble to the dock, climb in the boat and ski. To return, merely hit reverse: dock the boat, reload the car, drive to the plane, fly back to Chicago and walk up to the house.

My buddy Tullis saw our getaway sequence and said we had it made. I told him that for me, every stage brought responsibility and stress. How many times did I walk into work with my mind on plane safety, hangar rental deadlines, annual insurance? Then I'd shift to the lake. When are taxes due on the house? Did lawn maintenance show up? Is the boat clean for next weekend? Time to winterize. Then the main house: What about taxes there? Where are we with the contractors? My mind was an infinite loop about *stuff*, how to pay for it, how to maintain it, how to keep plates spinning.

Some people with far more than I ever owned take their possessions in stride, and I salute them. But I'm not like them. You ask, why not hire a manager? Because I'd have to manage the manager. The things that bought me a certain brand of happiness came with a high level of duty and angst.

What became my campaign to downsize our holdings had originated in Chicago, in my fortieth-floor office moment, when I pressed my forehead onto the desk and said there *had* to be more to life. As surely as I write this now, I believe God told me then to simplify. And while Lisa and I had known for some time that my exit from business would force us to downsize, until it began in earnest neither of us could have foreseen the freedom ahead.

To be sure, we did *not* hold a fire sale and embrace poverty. We subtracted ownership in ways that added to our time. As we did, I saw that my line between holding and letting go could be the line between debt and solvency, worry and calm, limitations and choices.

Some releases brought pain. The lake house. The convenience of popping up to Wisconsin's natural outdoor beauty. But those trips also drained my energy and focus. When I saw them as blockades to what I wanted more—access to God, to others, and to myself—I chose the bigger adventure.

I sold my airplane and, with tears in my eyes, flew it to Oklahoma. Then I jumped on a Southwest flight home with a Beech Bonanza–sized sense of relief, and with huge tracts of mental real estate thrown open for new development. When our boat sold with the lake house, two more big items disappeared, opening more brain cells for new business.

Those days I also was poring through a book called *Do More Better: A Practical Guide to Productivity,* by Tim Challies, in which he asks, "Ultimately, why did God create you?" and, "Why am I here?" The Bible says we're here to glorify God, to praise and point to him, which, in his economy, paradoxically gives us more of ourselves.

Challies defines productivity as stewardship of our gifts, talents, time, energy, and enthusiasm for the good of others and for God's glory. As I slipped by degrees into that groove, I found I liked it. Less mental clutter opened room for new priorities. My stress decreased. I was aware of feelings of joy. And joy is a key word.

In 2015, when *Time* magazine named its 100 Most Influential People, one was Marie Kondo, a Japanese organizing expert whose *New York Times* bestseller is titled *The Life-Changing Magic of Tidying Up*. That year before Christmas-clutter season, articles about her seemed to be everywhere, all repeating her mantra to keep only those things that spark joy.

That principle transfers to the life-changing magic of tidying our time. If the stress outweighs the joy, let it go. No one can tell you what stays or goes, but in the spirit of Marie Kondo, I can offer a few guiding questions:

1. Does it take up more time than you can justify?
2. Is it a financial drain?
3. Is it a physical drain, causing anxiety and stress?
4. Is it in any sense an idol, something that replaces God in your life? (Even fitness can become an idol when concern for your appearance trumps concern for your soul.)
5. Does it take time from your family?
6. Do you truly want it, or by chance do you own it to impress yourself or someone else?

Ownership cannot define joy. Our downtown condo was fun to bring up in conversation, and it gave us weekends in Chicago. But as Lisa and the kids understood that a month's taxes and association dues cost more than several days at the downtown Ritz Carlton—minus the maintenance—they got it. We could also *rent* beautiful lake places. And our large house with its basement dance floor, though great for entertaining, never felt like home. (With the surge in family time, however, came joy and the freedom to invest in relationships.)

Two caveats about housecleaning through all that you own. First, don't decide alone. Stay in conversation with your spouse and kids (if they're home) and your personal board of directors. (Much more to come on your board of directors.) Second, before you sell or give anything away, consider how else you might use it. When I flew people in my plane, opening hours to talk—or those times I could give emergency transit—good things happened. I could have done more of that, and now, several years later, I'm searching online for my old plane.

Lisa and I hardly qualify as poster children for a modest lifestyle, by the way. We drive nice cars—used, though, and without the new-car debt. We live in a beautiful home that is far from small but definitely more family-sized. The picture is never perfect, but I am more involved in my family and in primary relationships. I am more clear about my mission, more satisfied in the ways I can help others.

To wrap up the discussion on margin, while I was still in Chicago I visited some of the Wachovia Securities financial managers I had once worked with and what they said that day stayed with me. They said, "You're making 20 percent of what you used to and you're the happiest we've ever seen you."

7

Know Your Strengths

For decades Steve Smith (not his real name) was a top player in finance. On his first day at a Halftime Launch Event, he also was one of the most miserable people I've ever met. "I thought I had to renounce life as I knew it," he confessed in an early group discussion. In his grand housecleaning to begin to turn from success to significance, he'd also swept out all the things he did well. But wasn't that the point? Don't sacrifice and personal misery impress God and usher in significance?

Hold that thought.

In Steve's anti-joy service-and-sacrifice model, he sold his possessions and shuttered his top-drawer skills with money and people—basically everything he was hardwired to do. In Halftime-speak, he turned his back on his strengths, which *is* depressing. So depressing that his story quickly moved to the top of our list of illustrations about the importance of self-knowledge. Lack of it blows in a fog like the one in Steve's head. With it comes clarity, and the fog lifts. More to the point, when there's something you don't know, start with what you *can* know.

When you don't know how to begin your next stage of life, but you do know your personal makeup, start there: with God's fingerprints on your case.

In the last chapter we talked about making margin in your schedule—about creating time to pray, read, consult, talk, ponder, experiment, and more. A secondary benefit to those information-gathering techniques is that they dust for God's fingerprints. They uncover clues in your personality and in your proclivities, in books and Bible passages that speak to you, in your circumstances and choices, and in your relationships, for starters. As you begin to act on (or to rest in, as the case may be) the new information, you also gain specific insights into how you function, and when and where you function best.

So how do you begin to know your strengths?

Get the Book

Every new Halftimer arrives at the Halftime Institute with a list of his or her top five strengths because every new Halftimer has just completed the power-packed little exam in *Strengths-Finder*, a slender book by Tom Rath, mailed to them in advance. Note well that the title is *StrengthsFinder*, not *FaultsFinder*. If you've ever feared taking a close look inside yourself, you can relax because (1) if you're a believer, the worst of you is forgiven and redeemed, and (2) your *StrengthsFinder* results either affirm your current direction or help direct you to a better one.

Bob Buford built many a solid decision on Peter Drucker's advice to operate from "islands of health and strength." Bob and Peter used the principle in the context of choosing ministry partners, but I would stretch the meaning to include personal strengths. Don't lose precious time propping up your weaknesses, Peter was saying. Pour your energy and resources into what gins up results—and multiply those effects.

Seems obvious, doesn't it? And yet for some Halftimers the basic counsel to know their strong suits and play to them are shaky first steps on the road from paycheck dependency to personal freedom.

If you're beginning a Halftime journey, stop here. Do not pass "Go." Do not collect $200. Buy a copy of *StrengthsFinder* and complete the online quiz. See if knowing your dominant traits doesn't shine a headlight onto your patterns of thinking, your feelings and behavior, and why you do those things you do.

By the way, the strengths that surfaced in the test for Steve Smith of New York were obvious to everyone but him. (This is why you journey with a small group, and under a coach's guidance. More on that coming.) During a Halftime event, Steve's speaking skills shone. When he didn't have the floor he had us right in his palm, relating easily to people one-on-one. He was a natural salesman. He also acutely understood the financial markets.

After some effort from the Halftime staff, at the end of two days Steve gave himself permission to return to the brand of work he loved—fusing his financial skills and personal acumen to help men and women navigate money and life. Last I heard he was back at a major firm, flourishing, serving 1,500 clients.

Augustine wrote in his *Confessions*, "Our hearts are restless until they find their rest in thee." From the front lines of good intentions gone awry, Steve might add that our grand gestures mean little until we find our work in him.

My Years in the Fog

My own story is that when I learned through *StrengthsFinder* that my top five strengths are "relater" (not *realtor*), "harmony," "achiever," "developer," and "connectedness," I could look back and see a lifetime's clutter and confusion form a pattern of achievements, decisions, and dead ends.

Back in Chicago, in the fog years, other than wanting more status or financial value, I couldn't have said what motivated me. Unknown to me then, it was my achiever engine pushing me up the corporate ladder to fatten my net worth and accumulate more things.

One joyless piece of that rise was my superficial conversations with people I didn't know, all part of my job. The achiever in me pushed through, but the relater in me, I see now, was on life support. At the time all I knew to do was to work harder, though everything about those efforts still fit me like a suit three sizes too small. Looking back, I see that I was outside my strength.

Before I close this section, two more things about understanding how we are made. First is that as every person on a team is freed to be his or her best self, to work in the way he or she's created to work, productivity soars. At Halftime each one of us brings a strength pattern as unique as a DNA profile. As I said, I'm a relater. Our comfortable-at-the-cocktail-party guy has what *StrengthsFinder* calls "woo." Another is a deft connector of people and ideas. One is gifted with "individualization"— a keen aptitude for spying unique qualities in other people. One is an activator, turning ideas into action. And we have a learner, which every group absolutely requires. We complement one another. We also can be realists about each other's work styles and limitations, and how to manage them. This kind of intel helps in marriages, too, by the way, and in families.

Second, and this is an important part of the Halftime curriculum: every strength has a balcony and a basement, a lofty use and a low one. On the journey to know ourselves we learn whether we tend to apply a given strength with wisdom and in God's purpose—or selfishly. In Carmel, Madison, and Chicago, in my achiever mode, I could roll over anyone potentially blocking my path. And there were times that I did. That's my basement. Likewise, the "woo" strength of instant rapport can descend into manipulation. "Harmony," at basement level, operates as compromise or passivity.

As we add to our self-knowledge, we can also grow in basement-balcony awareness. In maturity, we spend the majority of our time upstairs.

You Can't Know Yourself By Yourself

Having just stressed that it's all-important, fundamental, etc., to know your strengths, I hurry to add that the knowledge is a tool and not a solution.

Your final life purpose emerges not in a day or in an assessment. Or in a heartfelt prayer—or even two. The life meaning you rightly look for is unlikely to arrive, *boom*, by epiphany. And that's the good news. It's in the journey, *your* journey, that good things happen. In the steps to know and learn, in the day by day, you are shaped, pruned, taught, revealed to yourself, and both softened and given wisdom. The journey prepares you for your arrival.

Just as important, it is impossible alone. From twenty years of helping men and women find their callings, we know for certain that on your own you grow tired, give up, or drift away. You fall to distractions that begin with "just this once." You overlook insights and feedback. You miss the people and relationships that make you grow.

Without your peers—the men and women who share your vision and values and challenges—you enter the valley of "surely life is more than this" (a healthy step) but never scale the mountain that leads to perspective and change.

Jeff Spadafora, Halftime's first and foremost expert on coaching—and recent author of *The Joy Model: A Step-by-Step Guide to a Life of Peace, Purpose, and Balance*—has a great illustration about the high role of peers in a Halftime journey. A man in a Halftime cohort (let's call him Ray) had taken the personal-profile exams and was stuck in knowing himself. More to the point, he was lodged in navel-gazing. Unable to figure out God's call, Ray's journey slowed to a crawl and then stalled out. No action. No "low-cost probes," which is Halftime terminology for getting out there and testing the waters.

In industry terms, what Ray needed was a swift kick in the pants. (Jeff's theory on Tiger Woods's very public marriage meltdown, by the way, is that he had no real friend to say to him, "What the heck are you doing?") But Ray was CEO of a 450-person company, and who's going to confront that guy? Answer: a man in his cohort—a fellow Halftimer who knew Ray and had his trust. During a meeting one day, a man burst out with, "Ray, I'm sick of hearing you bellyache. Go out and serve. For goodness sake, do anything."

Just as impressive, Ray heard him. Turns out Ray's eighty-year-old mother made sandwiches for the homeless every Tuesday at her church. The next Tuesday, for two hours, our navel-gazing CEO squirted mustard on baloney sandwiches while homeless men and women walked up and told him about their lives. At his next cohort meeting, Ray was bursting with new information.

"I don't know if you guys realize this, but a lot of these people don't choose to be homeless," he told his cohort. "A car breaks down and a guy can't get to work, and he loses his job, and the whole family's on the street. Or it's mental illness, and he has no backstop."

The men around Ray that day listened and nodded. In one small step of service, their friend made a giant leap in compassion. The breakthrough had opened not with making sandwiches, though, or by meeting the homeless. It started with Ray's willingness and risk, with exposure to "the things Jesus cares about." At the base, it started with the mystical powers of positive peer pressure.

We need accountability groups for the same reasons we set alarm clocks: because we know our limitations. The human brain at best has incredible capacity for rationalization—at worst, for self-delusion. Without the truth telling of people who know us, are *for* us, and would rather make us better than make us happy, we sleep in and miss the good stuff.

Another thing: if your work gives you any level of power or influence, you know the value of honest feedback and the difficulty, at times, of getting it. Some of your employees fear you, but most want to please you. When you smell trouble and ask questions, instead of bald truth, you get what that subordinate or associate thinks you want to hear. For you, honest criticism—both giving and getting it—is an art. And it's worth any trouble it takes to teach those around us, family and close friends in particular, that we want the hard news.

By now you may be thinking what I often think: that like bread and soft drinks, peers come in varieties and brands. We have peers in age and season of life, family situations, income, professional status, marital status. At Halftime we're convinced that, for your journey, your best peer group is not necessarily people your own age. Or those who match your affluence. Or men and women who share your social status, though all those markers can matter. On your halftime journey, it's maturity you want alongside you, and spiritual maturity in particular.

And yet. As quickly as I say "maturity," it won't be enough. Besides the life-giving input of fellow seekers, you absolutely require a guide with a road map. Besides regular meetings with a group of peers, therefore, we insist, *insist*, that our Halftimers also have a year (minimum) of one-on-one coaching.

Put Me in with a Coach

Several years ago, at a leadership team meeting, on a floor right below the Halftime offices, our then four full-time coaches stole away for an ad hoc conversation, and the topic quickly narrowed to dropouts. Popping up and down at a big table in a small room, the four men turned the room's whiteboard a rainbow of colors, all on one mystery: *Why do some Halftimers reach their goals while others drift away?* What makes some persevere and some disappear?

Why would type A men and women—high achievers, nonquitters, goal-oriented marketplace mavens—give up on anything, particularly on their dreams for significance?

Ideas that day flew, and early hunches fell away. The problem wasn't the Halftimers' schedules. Dropouts showed no consistent patterns related to study, prayer, low-cost probes, or any of the disciplines. The problem didn't trace to the state of a Halftimer's marriage or whether it needed help. Finances? Too much money or too little? Nope. No consistent factors in income or outgo were a reason to give up. As for faith, people of strong faith stayed in, and people of strong faith drifted out. No indicators there.

Still, a good number of Halftimers wound up ghosting their programs. There had to be an indicator. And there was. Interestingly, it was two-part. Part one was timing: Halftimers who abandoned their dreams did it in months five through eight of the program. Part two was coaching. Of all the people who saw their dreams through to completion, nearly every single person had stayed with a coach.

Of the people who had left, all had left coaching.

Why months five through eight? In the Halftime first-year journey, those are the months when dreams of a new season of life hit a patch of hard work, risk, sacrifice, and inconvenience. Egos take bruises. For a long time you've been king of the hill. Now you're trying new things and eating some humble pie. Instead of strategy, tactics, and execution, you're in a world of trial, risk, and some dead ends.

No question it's a tough go. The Halftimers who disappeared back into their old lives had drifted back into daily cares, or other lures, or standard-issue busyness. At some point it grew easier to revert to what they already knew, and to help other people by writing checks.

Bear with me for a quick aside. A woman I know volunteered at Parkland, Dallas's world-renowned indigent hospital. Early on she was assigned to surgery ER, where drug overdoses and gunshot wounds are another day at work. Needless to add, in that world, a volunteer's feelings are hardly high priority. On her second week at Parkland, taking a break from hustling up and down linoleum hallways, the woman called her friend to unload. "The doctors ignore me," she said. "No one here says a word except to tell me what to do. I'm on my feet from the minute I walk in. Tonight they had me cleaning up vomit."

In this case the complainer had a real friend. "I don't know if this is what you want to hear," her friend said, "but if you sign up to be a servant, you need to be willing to be treated like one."

And there's the rub. On the road to the sweet spot in God's plan, a leader is back to being a servant, back to informed guesses, dirty jobs, wounded vanity, and misunderstandings. The Halftimers who fall back and disappear feel beat down. Those who finish the footrace, who realize their dreams, are just as weary and beat down. The difference is that the finishers have the active involvement of someone who holds the big picture when they lose it. Somehow they keep moving.

"Do we treat cancer with aspirin or with chemo?" the coaches asked in their meeting that day. "People come to us wanting to make a change, and it's up to us to deliver best practice." Result: Halftime coaching now is mandatory, an ongoing relationship to get our world-changers past the inevitable dip.

And yes, since then, more Halftimers have persevered to engage in their next-season callings. But that also raises the question: Just what is it that coaches do?

The short answer, and it's hardly simplistic, is that they coach. Instead of taking a client's journey for them, coaches help Halftimers navigate the road for themselves. When the road doubles back or drops out of sight, the coach is there not with tidy answers or a to-do list but with the right questions. That's the power.

If you find a Halftime coach or ever become one, note well that it's not about having or needing to be a content expert. A Halftimer fearing a financial setback or struggling with marriage issues, for example, doesn't need you to forecast the money market or offer marriage therapy. He needs questions to help him see and understand the challenge for himself. "Is this a spreadsheet issue to run the numbers or something else?" "Is this a bump in the road for my relationship or time to see a counselor?"

The Halftimer's head is down to navigate details. The coach's head is up with an eye on the horizon. "What's really at the root of this?" a coach may ask. "What's driving this problem? What have you tried in the past? And what haven't you tried? Is this a practical issue, a spiritual issue, or some hybrid?"

Interestingly, a Halftimer who pierces through the confusion often finds shockingly simple solutions—a beautiful thing. Just as important, under a good coach, the Halftimer owns both the process and the outcome.

The three things to avoid in coaching are lack of ownership, wrong solutions, and potential for blame shifting. If you're wrestling with an issue and the coach solves it for you, you detach. Second, when a coach takes on the problem instead of your taking it on, you risk not getting to the real nature of the problem. Third, if the solution fails, the coach is the bad guy, and finger pointing is counterproductive.

Still the question hangs: Why should achievers need coaches in the first place? Of all people, aren't Halftimers most likely to be driven and self-motivated?

Twenty years of Halftime has an answer to that, too. Marketplace leaders rarely think systemically. Coming out of niche expertise, a business leader can spy nuanced connections between data, strategy, and execution—and entirely miss, say, the obvious links between values, parenting, and marriage. Also, it's a common truth that we humans have blind spots around unintended consequences.

Halftimers arrive thinking the journey is like starting up a new business. Just survey the opportunities, make a decision, run some due diligence, create a strategy, and execute. But beyond the business outline, their kids are on drugs, he's forty pounds overweight, and she's packing for a divorce. And it's dawned on no one to ask God for guidance.

The magic that happens among peers and between coach and Halftimer is truth. I can't stress that enough because with almost anyone, hard truth is at a premium. The nicer the person, often, the tougher it is to get it. Meanwhile coaches are full of stories about Halftimers bent on changing the world and unaware that their own worlds are falling apart. Coaches see the frightening ease with which a person can slap a Christian label on his or her own idea and fall into the delusion of "me making it happen for God." We forget that God doesn't need our help. He's not begging us to step in; he's offering an opportunity to partner with him, to be part of the good stuff.

The Real Conversation Is about Joy

We learn our strengths as we know ourselves. And knowing ourselves is nothing to attempt solo. When Ray's peer group pushed him into baloney sandwiches at the mission they moved him off a dead stop. Later his coach helped him understand what happened that day and use it to plan and execute next steps.

The real conversation, though, is about joy. People who come to Halftime for greater life purpose, for vocation and calling, are looking for joy. They know it has something to do with giving—but what kind? Where? To whom? And how?

We *think* the question is, "Do I sell my company and start an orphanage?" The answer may be yes; it may be no. You have to stay open to what's true for you. Your calling may be to make money and fund orphans. Or to train people to run orphanages. Or to be a spokesperson for children in need. Most people think they should be in frontline work when their real calling is in the home office. Or in public relations.

As the saying goes, you alone can do it, but you don't have to do it alone.

8

Know Your Spiritual Gifts

Our spiritual gifts are what God plants inside us to branch out through his work on earth—work that, according to Ephesians 2:10, has been waiting for us. Pretty exciting stuff. And if self-knowledge is power, knowledge of your spiritual gifts takes it to a new level.

Spiritual gifts are not personality traits like, say, extroversion or adaptability. They are not temperament labels like sanguine or phlegmatic. They are not aptitudes like having a mind for mathematics or words or sports. Think wisdom, hospitality, administration, discernment, healing, mercy, or teaching. In three different passages, the Bible lists some twenty-five gifts, although, interestingly, no two lists perfectly match, suggesting to me that the Holy Spirit stays flexible and creative as he outfits us for the kingdom.

To know our own spiritual gifts—and others'—plays out in ways both daily and practical. One well-known pastor will say that filling a church staff vacancy is not a question of, "Who has the skill to be efficient?" We should ask, he says, "Do these applicants use their skills to express reliance on the Lord? Do they use their skill to strengthen the faith and joy of others?" In other words, not just "can they do the work" but "does it tap into their spiritual gifts?"

Christians sometimes skirt discussing spiritual gifts because one or two of the gifts—tongues, in particular—tend to warm up conversations. Did I say warm up? *Heat* up. But *Trade Up* is about matching marketplace leaders with human need, and so we skirt the controversy and explore the issue. (For all heated points, I respectfully refer you to your denominational leaders, theologians, and pastors.)

To know your spiritual strengths, start with your church. Most congregations and denominations these days use gifts assessments to help place their members in ministries and outreaches. Barring that, visit online sites such as:

SpiritualGiftsTest.com

DesiringGod.org/messages/spiritual-gifts

PCUMC.info/pdf/SpiritualGiftsAssessment.pdf

Bruce Bugbee has an excellent book called *Discover Your Spiritual Gifts the Network Way*. However you learn about your spiritual aptitudes, when you know them, ask yourself five questions:

1. How do these compare and contrast with my *Strengths-Finder* results?
2. How do my strengths and spiritual gifts work together?
3. Which gifts resonate most deeply with me?
4. Which would I be most excited to leverage in my second half?
5. How might I use them more often and more effectively?

My Unofficial Spiritual Gift of Learning

My introduction to spiritual gifts was in the mid-1990s in a Bill Hybels series, and it electrified me. With every single person, our Maker was that fingerprint-specific? That first week, after the sermon, I dove into the Bible for myself to study these building blocks to Christian community. I also took my church's spiritual gifts assessment. In the car, using a hot new technology called cassette tapes, I heard pastors and teachers speak on the Holy Spirit and his work through us.

The new data recalculated major mental pathways in me. "What can I do for God?" I'd long asked. "What do I do well, or poorly? What do I like or dislike?" After years in the wilderness—in the *fog*—at last a GPS.

When my test results came, the three words—*discernment, wisdom,* and *encouragement*—stood out like old friends. *Of course.* How many closed-door conversations in my office and at our home . . . confessions from across a lunch table . . . sticky boardroom decisions . . . had turned on those three gifts? How many times had men and women far smarter than I opened up to me about complex personal or business-related problems? How many times had I heard the "I've never told this to anyone" or "I can't believe I'm telling you this" confession?

To *discern* is to know truth from error. A *wise* person applies knowledge to daily life. To *encourage* is to help a person see the truth of God's hope. Now when talk in my office grew confidential, I was aware of my spiritual aptitudes as well as my marketplace knowledge and strengths. Like a seal of approval, I knew that use of these abilities gave me joy.

In the way iCloud opens vast space to an otherwise small device, the Holy Spirit in me is my resource and capacity to serve others. My relater strength rolls out a welcome mat and invites trust. Discernment helps me guard that trust and respond with wisdom. Encouragement is the point.

I also began to see how my spiritual gifts snapped neatly alongside my marketplace strengths.

When Gifts Happen

My good friend George, advanced in age, had talked with his financial advisor and left upset. When George dies, his vast estate will divide among ministries dear to him—a prospect he relishes. The day before he and I visited, his financial advisor had urged him to delay giving for a full year after his death. George's attorney heard the advice and stiffened. Nothing doing, the attorney said; the will goes to work in the first six months.

George came to me, I believe, because a gift of discernment attracts people who need it. My decade or two in financial services didn't hurt. For more than an hour, George and I boiled down his complex questions and concerns. The longer it took to execute his will, I said at last, the bigger the financial advisor's take.

That night at home I ruminated. A few days later George and I met again, and I chose my words carefully. "George," I said, "the kind of things you said yesterday about your estate I hear from others your age. My professional hat is off now, and I speak as a friend. If you can live comfortably and still give money away, why wait for death? Why not share now and see the joy as you help outreaches and people rise to the next level?"

It came from my core. Joy and giving are the Halftime message. To give and then see the blessing . . . does it get any better? George, meanwhile, is a picture of understatement. Later that day he called to thank me with, "Whenever you're thinking about me, just keep thinking."

When a solution is bigger than I am, credit goes to the Holy Spirit, who directs those conversations. Talking to George I was in my strength as a relater, and in my spiritual gifts of discernment and wisdom. And I could draw on my financial career because God redeems everything.

I'll say it again: self-knowledge is power. In several parts of your Halftime journey you'll test the waters with different services, ministries, and outreaches. Opportunities abound and the needs are great, but not every cause will be your cause. Without self-knowledge, how can you know where you fit?

Strengths, Spiritual Gifts, and Joy

Way back in 2003, in Chicago, all I knew was that I wanted to serve God and that I cared about life's "castoffs." Having opened my schedule, I used Thursday afternoons to help homeless men and women write résumés. I loved the people, and yet in our time together I sensed an internal check. Was writing résumés the most I could do?

Two truths here. One, the work was right to do. Two, I was right to question it. Only a few years before, I had been the water-skiing, partying, corporate-climbing financial guy. Now I was a guy with "the least of these"—where Jesus is. The exposure not only introduced me to the nonprofit world, it helped shape my heart and mind for my ultimate fit at the Halftime Institute.

My next stop was Willow Creek, where I received an early volunteer assignment to work with special-needs kids and adults. This I also loved. *Loved*. Even now, on my own time, I work with challenged kids. But within my Halftime journey I had to ask: was this "It"? As full-time work, did it fully engage the ways God has wired me? All those questions, and my gut, kept me alert and led me on.

It's important to note here, *right here*, that this stage of "doing and not knowing" is where a lot of Halftimers lock up in paralysis through analysis. When that happens, follow the sage advice Ray received from his fellow Halftimer to "do something." Allow, even embrace, the uncertainty. Picture Mary—Jesus's mother—in a stable in Bethlehem as shepherds recount heavenly beings crowded across the night sky. What the young mother couldn't understand, she accepted in faith. In the not knowing, she "pondered these things in her heart."

Back at Halftime

This chapter on spiritual gifts closes with a snapshot about joy and work, two things originally intended to go together. In 2009, when I arrived at Halftime, I inherited directors who loved the Lord like no team I'd ever seen. More than once I saw them cry over the ministry. Whatever they were asked to do, they did, which is good, but to a point.

Lloyd Reeb, a *gifted* speaker, writer, and coach, at one time was asked to be president of Halftime, which he'd say would be a disaster. A strategy guy, a thought leader, is made for specific things. Greg Murtha, phenomenal with the strength of woo, also had been president. Another misfire. Seeing this devoted team too often at odds with their gifts, I asked each person, "What brings you joy?" Lloyd's joys were speaking, writing, and coaching. Greg's was talking to people about Halftime. Jeff Spadafora's was coaching. My joy was to get these people functioning in their joy, and that meant some repositioning.

In Christ's name, all ministry is noble and good. But not every good thing has your name on it.

9

Know Your Passion

Remember your dreams for humankind? I'm guessing they appeared to you in your late teens. Then came the hard light of careers, mortgages, and the next rung—and your dreams, mere sprouts, cooked to a crisp. At some early point our impulses to make a difference give way to the compulsion to make an impression. Our goals become security, admiration, and personal happiness. One day we look up and those early dreams are compost. And we're in a rut.

If any part of that includes you, join the teeming masses so set on Fifth Avenue inventory that they completely miss the goods with no price tag. One morning they blink and ask, where is my passion for What Matters, for what Jesus cares about? (Or maybe for anything.)

Passion, of course, comes in many brands. The passion of the Christ refers to the suffering he endured. In human terms, passion fills romance books that fill distribution-center warehouses and inspire movie scripts. For our purposes, passion refers to the driving human compulsion—until it dies of neglect—to fight tragedy, deprivation, pain, suffering . . . human wrongs. A great deal of that brand of passion, interestingly, comes out of our own pain.

Author Henri Nouwen titled one of his best-known books *The Wounded Healer*. After teaching at Notre Dame, Yale Divinity School, and Harvard, he left to work with mentally and physically handicapped people in Ontario at L'Arche, a place he helped put on the map. In *The Wounded Healer*, he ennobles whatever we consider our greatest shame. "The great illusion of leadership," Nouwen writes, "is to think that a man can be led out of the desert by someone who has never been there." God's most fertile ground, it turns out, is our wasteland—no matter how dark.

A good friend of mine, for most of his life, had given only passing thought to missing children. His life was too full and close to home. Then his seventeen-year-old daughter, Chelsea, out jogging one day, was abducted, raped, and murdered. To describe what such evil does to a parent needs a word far beyond nightmare. These mothers and fathers justifiably have a wide range of long-term reactions. Among other things, my friend was driven to right the system that failed his daughter.

Brent King's burning passion now is Chelsea's Law, part of a larger national campaign to strengthen the sentencing of sex offenders, increase awareness of their activities in public life, and limit their access to places where children congregate. His foundation also has put more than $300,000 into scholarships helping area high school students get to college.

In my life, the hollow ambition that drove my work and crashed key relationships—my years of wilderness—now fuels my passion to help others pull their heads out of their financial assets. When I read in *USA Today* about an empty executive—spouse detached, kids checked out, boatloads of money and accolades—my heart bleeds. I know that boat has a hole in it.

Along with Henri Nouwen, I know firsthand that people leaving the desert are profoundly fitted to retrieve those still in it. In North Carolina, Tana Greene was pregnant and married at age fifteen. By sixteen she was an emotionally and physically abused wife with no shelters to turn to. With her parents' help, she divorced at age seventeen and took control of her life. By twenty-nine, she was remarried and building her own staffing enterprise. Today as a business leader she serves on boards and organizations that, among other things, build women's shelters. A walking, breathing billboard for despair that leads to hope, Tana takes her passion, her story, to women high school age and older.

Halftimer Vince Leone ended eight years in the US Army disabled by combat and hobbled by another kind of disability in the civilian world. "I thought I was bigger than life and needed no help," he says. But post-deployment, a soldier is practically an orphan. Lack of mission drove Vince into his wasteland—a smoldering discontent that too many vets know.

For Vince the drought ended—and his mission began—at Christ's love. "The sin of the desert is when you find water and don't tell anyone," he says, and he began to mark his path for other vets. His Halftime coach, also a military veteran, stayed alongside as Vince formed VetStarts, a nonprofit drawing on the Halftime model to help men and women like him "find their way all the way home."

Just today I read about a woman who, pregnant with twins and diagnosed with a problem pregnancy, refused a specialist's advice to abort one of the fetuses. Now this mother of healthy twins and an adopted daughter champions special-needs adoption and orphan care.

The pain that births your passion also can come from someone else, by the way. Ed came to Halftime only with the sense that he had no purpose. But two hours into our first meeting, as he talked and we asked questions, we began to hear about his good fortune to have gone to a name university—and the tragedy of kids shut out of college. Why should doors open for him, he said, where others find dead ends? In a single afternoon Ed found his passion to help kids in poverty get into college.

Look In, Look Up, Look Around

Where is your passion? Look in, look up, look around. The journey winds through you, to God, and into your world. And the look into your world may be as easy as a week of reading *USA Today*.

You heard right: *USA Today*. Passion-challenged Halftimers are assigned to America's newspaper, Monday through the weekend edition, with orders to note what makes them (1) cry, (2) laugh, and (3) feel anger. (Just as important, they also note where they do not react.) As Halftimers scan and read, they jot down feelings and responses. Patterns emerge, questions surface, and right questions begin to unpack power.

I remember reading an article about Habitat for Humanity, builder of homes for the homeless, and admitting to myself that my desire to help the homeless ends at a construction site. Nothing about craftsmanship interests me. Nothing about hammers, levels, studs, or anything in a toolbox jibes with my strengths and gifts—all pertinent data. Another time I listened as a small group of former abuse victims described their childhood traumas. Tears ran down my cheeks; injustice stirs me more than almost anything. And yet, not once did I sense that this fight was my personal calling. Do either of those stories—Habitat for Humanity or hearing the abuse victims—make me unfeeling? They merely suggest that I'm wired to battle elsewhere.

Lloyd Reeb tells one of my favorite passion-discovery stories about a man who came to Halftime certain he had no compelling concern. He took the assignment to read *USA Today* and, two weeks later in a meeting with Lloyd, he threw the paper on the floor.

"It's a disaster," he said.

"What do you mean?" Lloyd asked.

The man shook his head. "Every single day, all I did was go straight to the sports section." And then Lloyd tipped the ball in.

"That's it," he said, stating the obvious. "Your passion is around sports." And the man who found the *USA Today* sports section like a heat-seeking missile now heads an athletic program for inner-city kids.

The heart is unknowable even to ourselves, *especially* to ourselves. But though my heart often is opaque to me, I believe I can sit with someone else and in thirty minutes see what drives that person to be sad, glad, or angry. She may come in talking about politics, but beneath headlines, legislation, stats, and energy are hurting people with real needs—and a cause that makes her heart leap. Passion has everything to do with loving God and loving my neighbor as myself.

Jesus was in a crowd one day fielding questions when a lawyer stepped in to trip him up. Bible paraphraser Eugene Peterson picks up the story from the gospel of Mark:

Hearing the lively exchanges of question and answer and seeing how sharp Jesus was in his answers, he put in his question: "Which is most important of all the commandments?"

Jesus said, "The first in importance is, 'Listen, Israel: The Lord your God is one; so love the Lord God with all your passion and prayer and intelligence and energy.' And here is the second: 'Love others as well as you love yourself.' There is no other commandment that ranks with these." (Mark 12:28–31 MSG)

The "others" that Jesus loved form a deceptively simple list that has inspired uncountable ministries, outreaches, and opportunities. We bring out that list as Halftimers consider the field before them. Jesus told us to:

- Feed the hungry (Matt. 25:35)
- Give drink to the thirsty (Matt. 25:35)
- Give hospitality and shelter to the stranger/foreigner/ refugee (Matt. 25:35)
- Clothe the naked (Matt. 25:36)
- Care for the sick (Matt. 25:36)
- Visit the imprisoned (Matt. 25:36)
- Help the widows and orphans (Ps. 82:3; Isa. 1:17; and especially James 1:27)
- Provide justice to the oppressed and disenfranchised (Matt. 5:38–45; Mark 10:42–45; Luke 4:18–19)

This list is hardly a call to sell everything, give the profits to charity, and reduce your wardrobe to sackcloth and ashes. It's a call to find hurting people in our schools, banks, factories, department stores, country clubs, movie studios, and hospitals. Stay open, wide open, to what can be. If your call is to feed the hungry and you are a schoolteacher, it may be as simple as fine-tuning to student needs. Your call to help widows and orphans may be as an estate planner. You may head a business that creates jobs for the poor.

Also, never mind whether anyone officially knows that your work is where you serve God. The One who matters knows. And the ways he can use you are as endless as he is great.

On the Other Hand

In a given cohort of Halftimers, more than half arrive believing they have no passion. In the remaining half, a good percentage find it hard to narrow their passions to just one. Or to a handful. To them I say that while we may have many compassions, our driving passions form a short list.

The difference is the Holy Spirit, and in my experience his guidance comes in (1) listening to him and trying to obey, (2) an unforced way (versus my trying to make it happen), and (3) unexpectedly.

To begin to hear the Holy Spirit, during my Halftime I began something new and foreign to me (which gets its own chapter later in this book). Alone, in quiet, and free of outside distractions, I began to ask, "Speak to me," after which I would sit, listen, think, and write. No reading, not even the Bible. In our era of nonstop sound, I turned the dial to silent and gave God the floor.

This solitude, with no reading, builds on time spent in Scripture—time when I submit to truth bigger than I am. I bring that up because for a believer wanting to follow God, the operative word is "submit." If that's difficult for you, be aware that at various times it is for any believer. To start, as you read Scripture (try the Gospels or Psalms), consider how to submit in just one or two ways. Assume that what you read is true, and ask how you can apply it in your heart and life.

One place to start is the Lord's Prayer, both deceptively short and infinitely rich. Speak it through line by line, and consider how to grow in a child's love ("our father"), worship ("hallowed be thy name"), awareness of the holiness around you ("thy will be done on earth as in heaven"), daily dependence ("give us this day our daily bread") and giving up the "right" to ever take offense ("forgive us our sins as we forgive others").

My coach, Jeff, came to God as an adult after years of thinking of the Bible as an attempt to brainwash people. As a new Christian he would read it looking for loopholes in the logic, expecting a prescription for a "fuddy-duddy lifestyle." He stayed at it, however, and found himself wanting to know, "What did Jesus really say? Who is God? And what did he say about how to live out our time on earth?" Because his previous life lacked deep joy, Jeff gave the Bible a chance. Now he says to Halftimers: "What happens is, when you've tried it your way and the joy you want never comes, you pay some attention to this counterintuitive stuff. And it actually works."

By the way, for Jeff and for me, time hearing from God has yet to involve a meditative state and/or sudden enlightenment. Or voices. Or thunder. And yet it changes a person and it changes our lives.

Jim Smith (not his real name) lost his dad when he was ten and, understandably, he grew up angry at God. The few times he approached faith in God, he got bitten. Like the time he looked up "death" in a Bible and read, "Let the dead bury the dead." How could a loving God say that? More "bad reading" threw up more barriers, and as an adult Jim needed years to unwind from around the wrong axle. The moral is, if you don't understand the Bible, don't be quick to toss it. Just read in a group study or with a friend who knows it better than you do.

While we're on it, as much as it's in your power, find a church that has the music, teaching, people, and resources that resonate with you and how your brain operates. Shop around till you do. That's a big part of finding your passion and fanning it.

My second point about hearing from the Holy Spirit is that his work is unforced. If you feel yourself straining to manufacture a right outcome, drop it. But when something supernatural or unexpected comes out of left field . . . well, that's my third point. I've concluded that when supernatural events take place, or something completely unexpected happens, it can only be of the Holy Spirit. And I pay attention.

In Chicago, as Lisa and I took our first steps to leaving my career in finance, out of the blue came a call to buy our home. This was during a housing crisis, and five other homes were up for sale on our street. Ours was not for sale. The buyer paid 10 percent over what we'd paid and skipped the inspection. We closed within thirty days.

At the time I couldn't have told you what was happening. Lisa and I just tried to obey. We said to each other, "If they're willing to pay above what we paid, and in this market, we should do it." And we did.

Months later we were in our new home and attending the Halftime event in California. As I wrote earlier, at that event Halftime's Tom Wilson asked to visit us in Chicago, and that night Lisa dreamed I would be CEO of Halftime. Through the next months as we talked with Tom on and off about a leadership position, I began to pray, as did Lisa. *Is this the right decision for our family?* I believed the Holy Spirit was at work. And then, though our new home was not on the market, our realtor relayed an offer. Remember the economy in 2008 and '09? And the buyer paid cash.

This is not to spotlight the great fortune of Dean and Lisa Niewolny but to humbly submit that supernatural, unexpected things can indeed happen as we gain "eyes to see and ears to hear." For Lisa and me, this was a huge signpost on the journey to trust the Lord at work in our lives.

Looking back at dots that would become a picture, if you were to ask, "How do you know when it's the Holy Spirit?" I'd say, "It becomes obvious."

This is the passion chapter, but the key is trust. Trust the Holy Spirit both to open doors and to reveal what you are made to do. And remember, when it's supernatural, you may have to work, but you won't have to force it.

10

State Your Mission

Why take the trouble now to channel your strengths, spiritual gifts, and passions into a mission statement of fifty words or fewer? Because of situations like Rick's (another fictitious name).

After years in business, and after considerable back and forth with his Halftime coach, Rick had a spot-on second-half mission statement: one sentence captured his gifts, his target group, and his goals for them. In it, he made no mention of finance. He was a natural mentor, and in his second half he wanted to walk alongside young men in their decision-making years.

One more thing, though: one of Rick's strengths was "achiever." Set a goal for him and somewhere in his psyche a muscle would twitch. His pastor, knowing of his success-to-significance journey, also knew of the muscle. Understand-ably, the pastor asked Rick to head the church's next capital campaign. And to the amazement of many, most notably to himself, the Halftimer said no . . . followed by, "Let me tell you why."

"I've worked hard to know what God's called me to do in this next season of life," he said. "In the next year I plan to invest in four young men, and several more the next."

Whoa. Checking back with his coach, Rick still felt dazed. He said, "I rejected something I could have done well for the thing God called me to. Now I'd better get the mentoring right because I just turned down my pastor."

In his first of what would be many mission-statement moments, Rick drew a bright red line between calling and competency. There's the trick. When you open your life to service, you're open season for people representing many good causes. If you seriously pursue your Ephesians 2:10 calling, brace yourself for a wave of calls, options, information, and offers. When it happens, as it did with Rick, the difference between method and madness is to have a mission statement and use it.

Rick's coach is Halftime COO Paul McGinnis, a perceptive guy who compares this stage of the Halftime journey to having a thousand-piece puzzle dumped on your desk. "You think you can never complete it," he says. "At best you're wondering, 'What is the size and scope of this next thing I'm doing?'"

As with any jigsaw, Paul says, first you build the borders. "The corners are your strengths, gifts, and passions," he explains. "The edges are your constraints, your limitations. A physical problem, maybe, or elderly parents."

Some people try to isolate one puzzle piece out of the thousand—say, the one to get the kids through college, or work with a spouse who doubts the whole program, or determine whether to leave a job—and work the whole picture from there. But say no to that one-piece idea. Your second-half calling comes not in a single response, or decision, or feeling, or question. It's an entire picture combining your gifts, the group you want to serve, and the goal of your service.

Let's talk about those.

Writing Your Mission Statement

In your short, sweet-spot statement of purpose, your strengths, spiritual gifts, and passions come together in a single answer to three questions.

1. **Gifts.** What are my strengths?
2. **Group.** What group do I want to serve?
3. **Goals.** What outcome do I wish to see?

To prove that brevity is possible, this thirty-two-word example joins all three categories: *To use my entrepreneurial skills to create training and jobs for women coming out of prostitution so that they can become financially self-sufficient, connect in community, and grow mentally, socially, and spiritually.*

On the front end, mission statement drafts are wordy and unwieldy. That's as it should be. When getting ideas down, say everything that comes to mind. Once it's all down, look for repetition and extra words. Consider where you can condense ideas. Draft rewrites. Stay at it until, in fifty words or fewer, you can state your strengths, your target mission group, and your desired outcome. Besides making your mission easy to memorize and bring to mind any time, brevity forces clarity. And clarity sweeps out confusion.

We tend to hide behind extra words. A national legal-writing expert tells attorneys until they can state their case in seventy-five words or fewer they don't know it. And getting to those seventy-five words (or fewer) may take a day or more. Blaise Pascal is credited with saying, "If I'd had more time I'd have written a shorter letter." And it's all true. Brevity takes time. And until you can state your mission, you can't reach it.

My twenty-four-word mission statement is *"to inspire and encourage high-capacity leaders on a journey to identify their Ephesians 2:10 calling and engage in the issues Jesus cares about."*

In terms of the three-question outline, it checks through: I want to use my spiritual gifts of inspiration and encouragement because this brand of helping people is a strong source of joy for me. It's how I'm made. "High-capacity leaders" is the group I serve best as a wounded healer—and it revs my engines. As a former marketplace leader, I know power's lures and its dead ends. I know the freedom of serving God instead of money. I know that a marketplace leader who realizes her or his Ephesians 2:10 calling can re-leverage those skills to sky-high effect.

My intended outcome is to see others come into their strengths on behalf of the people Jesus cares about—orphans, widows, the imprisoned, and the poor, for starters. In God's economy, in serving others' needs we enrich ourselves.

Bob Buford's statement came from his friend and coach Peter Drucker. They'd known each other for maybe eight years when Peter pegged Bob's mission in a single sentence. "At this stage in your life," he said, "your job is to transform the latent energy of American Christianity into active energy."

Bob held onto the phrase, though for a while he didn't quite get it. Sometime later he was walking down a road in East

Texas when two synapses connected and . . . *bingo.* Grabbing a Winston cigarette carton off the ground, Bob scribbled Peter's words on the inner wrapper.

For Bob, the first official halftimer, this statement of purpose turned a light on what he'd so far done by instinct. He'd founded Leadership Network to help pastors scale their churches to the needs they served, and he'd founded the Halftime Institute—the university for the second half of life. Now, inside a cigarette carton, two passions aligned. Bob's job wasn't to stir up leaders or pastors with new energy. It was to help them release and direct the firepower already in there. Facilitation was Bob's gift. These were his groups. Here was the outcome. For everything that came after, this mission statement pointed to Bob's true north.

One more thing. Because Bob is, in my observation, a natural teacher, he distilled Peter's generosity of spirit in his life into the four things every good coach should try to give: permission, encouragement, applause (or course correction), and accountability.

Specificity Is Everything

Peter Drucker says a mission statement defines our purpose, why we do what we do. Bob says a mission statement answers two important questions:

- In light of my unique design, what do I believe is my highest and best contribution in advancing the cause of Christ on this earth?
- In what direction is God leading me to invest my talents, time, and treasure?

In Bob's case, the answers were:

- To use my leadership skills and relationship networks to turn the latent energy of American Christianity into active energy.
- To be a thought leader, via writing and speaking, in mobilizing marketplace leaders for kingdom impact.
- To use my business skills to help churches run more efficiently and effectively.
- To transform my business into a ministry that spreads God's love to my employees and customers.

In your own mission statement, in every case, at all times, without fail, be specific. *To use my gifts and strengths to help people in Jesus's name* is not specific. When you need a filter to discern best from good, a statement like that will be a sieve.

Here's an example of getting it right. In 2014 at a Halftimer Launch Event, a pharmaceuticals exec named Scott Boyer wrote that his mission was "to create a sustainable not-for-profit foundation-owned branded generic pharma company to reallocate two-thirds of the profit margin so that under-resourced epilepsy patients in the United States and the rest of the world can receive appropriate pharma care."

No mention of Scott's gifts, but from nearly thirty years in Big Pharma—Abbott Labs, Bristol-Meyers Squibb, and inVentiv Health—his marketplace skills shine out. Likewise, the statement shines with simplicity from hard thinking. Scott intends to help the epilepsy patients who fall outside of wealthy or emerging markets—men and women and children with no market equity—and he intends to make the aid sustainable.

I love that Scott never considered missions per se. His mission "group" came to him one day on a graph chart showing pharmaceutical distribution to wealthy countries and to ROW—"rest of the world." The acronym haunted him. He thought about, in his words, "the millions of under-resourced patients who could be easily treated by low-cost medications if only they had access."

To treat suffering and silence with medicine on a mission, Scott set his first target group as people with epilepsy. Ultimately he sees a future "when effective diagnosis and life-changing treatments will be available to ALL people, at ALL times, in ALL the world."

"All great for ol' Scott," you may be thinking. "But how do I write a specific statement when I have no sense of what group I'm here to serve?"

Draw a Picture

If that's the case, it's time for you to draw—to get into a brain lobe that operates beyond words. On a sheet of paper or a whiteboard, your assignment is to sketch, even with stick figures and bad outlines, anything that comes to mind about your gifts, your desires, what moves you . . . and see what appears. Repeat: no words.

Drawing is standard Halftime procedure, and one of my favorite whiteboard-to-world stories is Dale Dawson, a Halftime poster child who actually did trade a corner office for central Africa. It started with a Rwandan clergyman's visit to Dale's church in Arkansas. Years later, Dale was in Rwanda, by now a second home, pouring his marketplace-honed "maximizer" strengths into nation building. You may remember back to

1994 when four months of genocide wiped out eight hundred thousand people in Rwanda, obliterating its soul and its infrastructure. After a decade of trial, error, and hard-won lessons, Dale saw that he could best serve Rwanda long term, and sustain that help, by investing in the country's best and brightest high school graduates. Since then, each year, Bridge2Rwanda cherry-picks thirty to forty of the country's top students for an eighteen-month gap program to study abroad. After the schooling, B2R stays with the students another five years as they find and secure careers back in Africa.

"In microfinance or education, to keep giving to the poorest, and only that, is to extend dependence," Dale says, echoing the Druckerism to build on islands of health and strength. "To change a society to care for itself, you build into the promise and strength of its talent."

And it started with a drawing, not even a good one.

"Bob insisted every person needed a mission statement and told us to express it on the whiteboard," Dale recalls. "No words allowed."

At the time Dale had no use for mission statements, but there he was drawing an outline of Africa and, to its left, an outline of the US. Between the two, he drew a connecting line, an arc. "What gives me joy, what I feel called to," he said that day, "is to build a bridge between the US and Rwanda, and to transform lives at both ends." Bingo.

Is it growing clearer that passions come to a person in as many ways as there are people? Scott Boyer was haunted by a corporate sales graph. Dale Dawson, against his better judgment, drew a picture. Bob Muzikowski, founder and head of the Hope Foundation in downtown Chicago, rode the L train to work every day, and every day saw inner-city kids hanging on street corners. His passion became one of the largest inner-city Little League organizations in the country.

And If That Doesn't Work?

Okay, suppose you're still the exception. You're at a whiteboard and still nothing. In that case, choose a weapon—one or more:

1. **Write.** Write a story of when you were lost in the pleasure of using your gifts. Then, preferably with a peer group or coach, review it for clues.
2. **Ask.** Go back to your peer group for ideas and input.
3. **Read.** Return to *USA Today* articles, to what makes you glad, sad, or mad (or bored).
4. **Confer.** Spend time with your coach, who should ask you informed questions.
5. **Confide.** Talk with someone you trust about your greatest pain.

J. T. Olsen, now head of a ministry called Helping Hands, lost both his mother and father in a car crash when he was only fourteen years old. Talking with his Halftime coach, he discovered that his greatest hurt also was his greatest passion. Helping Hands connects—what else?—orphans and families. Back to the power of a wise listener. A coach can hear someone like J. T. for ten minutes, get to his tears for orphans, and open him to his own passion.

One closing note on the sometimes extra-long road to your passion and your mission. When a Halftime journey feels labored, we learn, time and again, that no labor is in vain. The journey prepared that Halftimer for her or his destination, and the journey never fails. Everything you learn has value. Be encouraged. Over time a picture, a phrase, or a feeling will come, and your page will turn.

The Elephant in the Room: Does God Want to Move You to Africa?

But will God move you to Africa? How many Halftimers' biggest fear has been that God relocates them to a developing continent? Do big moves happen? Yes. Often? *No.* In fact, what we hear most are comments like, "Wow, as a financial attorney, I never thought of all the ways my clients need this insight."

One Halftimer, a Lowe's executive, came to us looking to make a dramatic move. And during his Halftime launch event, he identified his love for the homeless. When he learned, however, that Lowe's had a share of homeless employees, a light went on. He said to us, "My work for the world is right here in my own company."

Some 60 percent of Halftimers stay where they are with new sense of mission, new information on themselves, and new joy. My word to you on what to expect is straight from Jesus in John 10:10, where he contrasts his role as shepherd to that of a thief. It's your promise. "The thief comes only to steal and kill and destroy," he said. "I have come that they may have life, and have it to the full."

PART 3

THE DESTINATION

We are God's handiwork, created in Christ Jesus to do good works, which God prepared in advance for us to do.

Ephesians 2:10

11

Populate Your Journey

Not long ago a former Halftime coach had a massive heart attack. When it happened he *already* was in a hospital for an unrelated treatment. From even five minutes away he would never have made it.

As the saying goes, death has a way of focusing the mind, and this former coach told another coach later that in the moment of his heart attack, only two things mattered: Jesus and relationships. All the ministry stuff is great, he said, but if those two things get lost, it ain't worth it.

Halftime could fill a bookshelf with cautionary tales about priorities, but that one should do it. After Jesus, our relationships are everything, and really, Jesus and relationships are inseparable. The path to our Ephesians 2:10 calling, to the work God prepared us for, winds through people. Period. No discussion. No detours. The journey to significance taps into our deepest relationships, and on that journey we must build—or rebuild—primary life connections.

I say "rebuild" because almost no one excels in the market-place without close-range collateral damage: lack of intimacy, lack of presence. And when life happens—when a job ends, a big birthday hits, death or an accident happens, the medical news is grim, a divorce slams in, retirement arrives—it's no longer about living the dream. You're in the valley of the shadow of death with no GPS, no flashlight, no one to walk beside you.

If any part of that rings true for you—if you've isolated yourself and you know it—the good news, ironically, is that you're in good company. And you're due for a comeback.

Steve Ivaska, a former Caterpillar, Inc. exec, would be the first to tell you that his relational life has an Old and New Testament: law and grace. The dividing line came on December 26, 2009, when his 1,100-mile running goal for the year was short by 16 miles. (Yes, his strengths assessment includes an "achiever" theme.) That midwinter day while his wife took care of kids and grandkids and prepared lunch for fifteen, Steve took to the neighborhood streets.

Then, just blocks from home, Steve went down on frozen ice beneath the snow. Minutes before he'd been tying shoelaces in a warm room. Now he was on all fours begging God to keep him from passing out. His broken (and dislocated) right ankle would land him on a path he'd soon define for himself as two questions: *How much time do I have left? And what am I going to do with my time?*

As his leg healed, Steve looked around and found himself short on anyone to talk to. For decades emotional detachment had been almost his badge of honor. His wife he had long looped out of his top priorities. At work he was a "functioning extrovert" to mask what he knows now was deep uncertainty that he belonged there. Now as he weighed whether to leave CAT or stay another five years, his closest conversations were not with his wife, a friend, a brother, a pastor, or a counselor . . . but with his financial advisor.

"We learn to look as if we know what we're doing or can figure it out," Steve says now to the leaders he mentors. "As a result, certainly in my case, our relationships stay on the surface. I had a lot of friends but few close ones."

But people who do the hard work to catch up also seem to pull ahead. With his ankle propped and his mind newly open, Steve began to run through books on finance and retirement. Someone handed him *Halftime*, which led him to enroll at a Halftime program and get a coach. Digging deeper into his relationship with God, he came across 1 Thessalonians 1:3, in which Paul commends believers for their journey of faith, their labor of love, their endurance inspired by hope in Christ.

That day for Steve, a passage stood up and walked off the page. "Faith is a journey?" he thought. "Then I don't have to have it all figured out?" He absorbed that. Then "labor of love" hit him like a two by four. God all but said aloud, "You blow by people on your way to the next meeting, the next project, the next whatever. No time for anyone. But I want you to love people—at CAT or anywhere—and without that love I can't use you."

Steve remembers nothing different after that. But Sundays in the lobby after church his wife was hearing from people, "He's never spent time with me. Now he's got all the time in the world."

As Steve also moved toward knowing his wife again, her responses both stung and healed. Once, in the car together on a trip out of a national park, he asked for her opinion on something. After a pause she said, "For so many years you set the bar so high in your life that I thought I could never measure up. I'm still unsure if it's safe to enter into conversation with you."

"It's not easy seeing the damage as God peels back my life," Steve says now. "Yet when I share these struggles with the men I coach and mentor, they open up too."

This chapter looks at how the Halftime journey takes us, as it did Steve, into real friendships. While it's true that friendships have no hard-core survival value, in C. S. Lewis's words they are what give value to survival. Amazon distribution centers must ship acres of books by the week on how to get relationships, mend or deepen the ones you've got, decode their languages . . . and it all matters. For our purposes, the Halftime journey concentrates on three categories of human connection:

1. Intimacy with your spouse
2. Friendship with peers
3. Interaction with your personal board of directors

No question many other relationships are essential. Your kids, for starters, rank alongside your spouse. But on your Halftime journey these three categories of human bonds—as they form, build, or repair—stand to be your chief sources of honesty and growth.

You Need Your Spouse

One of the most important and shortest talks I ever had with Bob Buford was in 2008. I'd come to the Halftime Institute fired up, ready to conquer the world, and found myself in a chair next to his. I said to him, "Lisa's not where I am on this. I'm ready to go, and she's not there."

Bob said, "Stop, then. Do nothing until you're equally yoked."

Really? When God's calling me? "It'll turn into a disaster," Bob said, which froze me. Lisa and I are husband and wife, as if I needed a reminder. When we disagree, it means I can't race ahead without her. (It also reminds me that, disagree, agree, or draw, I must always be in prayer for her.)

As all spouses discover, marriage yokes us to people with their own interests and callings. My calling is to help high-capacity men and women find their Ephesians 2:10 calling. Lisa loves girls, pageants, the arts, dancing, acting—a pageant winner herself, she's helped guide many young winning contestants. On that platform she's about seeing young girls fall in love with Jesus and seize their potential. Needless to say, until I met Lisa those things were off my radar, but I can be interested if she is. And she puts up with my baseball, football, and plenty more.

In relationships, genuine interest in the other person is a high form of love. The key in the lock is to relearn or learn to ask questions and then hear the answers. And then ask a follow-up question. A good opener, as Steve Ivaska discovered, is "What do you think?" When difficult topics surface, go ahead and lean in. In every case keep your spouse's agenda ahead of yours. This counterintuitive advice is not just relationship nutrition, by the way; it's what God tells us to do.

In his coaching, Jeff tells each of his clients to go to their spouses with a three-part question: What are your dreams for one year, three years, and ten years from now? Answer each one on three levels: for you as a child of God, for us as a couple, and for us as a family.

Get all nine responses and go to dinner, Jeff says. Pop open a bottle of wine and read through the answers. Unlike a workplace assignment with a hard deadline, by the way, getting to a thoughtful response can take time. Wives especially, if they have poured themselves into raising kids, tend to bury their own dreams. Still, a marriage on life support is hardly a gender thing—it's human. Whether you're male or female, if you're an achiever, for years your drink of choice has been challenge and success, and you've been feverishly hoping the next glass would bring more joy or happiness. Welcome to sobriety.

In my own marriage of imperfect partners, Lisa and I know that without constant communication—and transparency and trust—we flounder. And it happens before we know it. Hard-driving men and women skip the time it takes for authentic conversations at home to put in more time at work. Or as we immerse ourselves in work, the person at home appears less valuable than someone who can push us up the workplace ladder.

At the same Halftime event where Bob told me to wait to be in sync with Lisa, he told the group that an all-time top decision in his life had been to come home every day and, for at least fifteen minutes, hear about Linda's day. His job was to say nothing. (I still work on that part.)

At first Bob found himself wanting to break in with commentary and news from his own day. But listening is a muscle, and it can build. As Bob grew familiar with Linda's days, her goals and interests, his own interest grew. For her part, Linda felt cared about, validated. And their marriage showed it.

For myself, when I talk about marriage, I tend to use words like *authentic* and *openness* because they're foundational—and because my "harmony" strength can work against them. Instead of getting conflict on the table with Lisa, I tend to shove difficulties under the rug. On those days when she and I get it right, when we take on the hard stuff together, we benefit from transparency and forgiveness. We also benefit from knowing each other's hot buttons and working around them. I can't stress that enough.

A couple more tips that I need to write down again for myself and tape to the bathroom mirror: when we pray together—for that matter, when the kids join us in prayer—we're never stronger. We bond in wanting each other's best. Then there's date night: time apart to remember to laugh and have fun. In the work-and-children-only rut our marriage drops out of sync. We look up and, as when I drive off course, we have to work to recalibrate.

Lloyd Reeb is an A-1 Halftime coach who also counsels his clients to put their spouses first. One day after talking to Lloyd, Tim Patton, a board member at Halftime, realized he knew too little about his wife's interests. At home that evening, Tim said, "Honey, I want to know your passions and desires for the rest of your life." Later as he tried to report on their conversation to a Halftime group—his wife standing next to him—Tim couldn't speak for the tears. It went that well. Since then the Pattons' adult kids have seen their dad, thirty-four years into the marriage, honor their mom in a whole new way.

But what about the other reaction? What happens when the spouse you work to put first still shows no interest in your Halftime journey, and no desire to serve God? One part of the resistance may be information. When spouses don't "get" what you're thinking or doing, imagination can run wild. Will the family lose its home while you have a midlife crisis? The answer is that when misunderstandings reign you decide nothing. So you talk. Openly and transparently. If you're out of practice talking, just start where you are.

In Halftime's early years (remember, this was the type A's leading the type A's) we taught little on the heart journey. Our unspoken motto was to get people to "do something." Get out there, figure out your Ephesians 2:10 calling, and get busy. By the early 2000s we knew that an Ephesians 2:10 calling without a spouse's endorsement is a wrong number. Or as Bob put it to me that day at my first Halftime event, it's a disaster.

Bottom line: until your spouse is for it, it's not God's call. My yearning to "do something" began in 1999. Not until 2009 were Lisa and I equally yoked, on the same page, and not until then did I fully sense God's perfect timing.

As a type A, you think you know when you're ready to move. As a believer and spouse, you're not free to act alone. Meanwhile, the journey to your spouse's endorsement—or not—prepares you for the final destination. You'll see that looking back. And it makes you a better marriage partner.

You Need Friends

Most new Halftimers arrive in our offices with few friends—often none—and no one to confide in. At first that shocked me. Growing up in baseball, I was always in a group. Even when they were contributing to my delinquency, my buddies were in my life. My walk with God had come through a friendship—in that case, with Paul Wilson. Yet for most leaders, by midlife, high-stakes busyness has crowded out heart-level connections, and by they time they get to Halftime, the deficit shows.

A second reason we reach midlife with no friends, something Steve Ivaska alluded to, is the imposter syndrome. If you're unsure of yourself at work and everyone else seems to have it together, it'll be a cold day somewhere before you open up. In technical terms, the primary cause of your emotional isolation is thinking you're the only idiot that doesn't get it.

Meanwhile the Halftime work to get you to your true self runs on involvement with peers and the guidance of a coach. So if you're starting from zero to add people to your life, a reasonable and important first step is to get in a group. Start with people likely to share your desire for a life with meaning. And give yourself margin for mistakes. Look into church options—a Bible study or book group. If you have no church, visit a couple. A visit is not a blood pact to join. It's another low-cost probe. At work in Chicago I learned about Halftime when I joined a Halftime Huddle—seven or eight guys meeting every week to go through the book together. *Boom*: common ground, and an open door into conversations necessary to my mental survival.

We emphasize common ground because that's where friendships take root and grow. C. S. Lewis, in a classic chapter in his book *The Four Loves*, says friends are born as one says to another, "What! You too? I thought that no one but myself . . ."[1]

If you're ready for it, ask a few people if they'd want to go through a book together. Not all will say yes, but some may. The asking takes initiative, but you're not this far into a book about changing your life because you lack initiative.

A guy on our team for years wanted not necessarily a Bible study, but a circle of men to look at life together through the lens of the Bible, to set goals and help each other grow. But he put it off. One day his wife came back from a prayer walk on the beach and said to him, "I know you're supposed to form that group," which got him off his duff. He talked to nineteen guys, men he admired for things like their faith, their business expertise, their marriages. And he set the bar high: meetings the first Friday of every month for two years, only two misses a year allowed. When he approached men with the idea, of the sixteen who said yes, fourteen told him they were craving it. Two, when they heard the invitation, cried. Every man who said yes was desperate for help and relationships, but someone had to step out and start it. At the eighteen-month mark, the group stabilized at eleven guys.

Steve Ivaska prayed about starting a group of younger men. When he approached several and laid out expectations, everyone he talked to was busy. Except one. That guy said, "Ashley and I have been praying for mentors for the last three years." That sealed the deal, and the two men got started. (Several others would join.) Remember dating? It's like that. To assemble a group, or just start friendships, you approach likely candidates and trust God for right connections.

The fine print on the friendship warning label is that as you get into one or a few friendships, you'll run into unexpected parts of yourself. Lisa said to me one day, "You never used to cry. Now you cry all the time." In my thirties I had no tears. In my fifties, and with people I trust, they just come. Friends stir up authenticity and authenticity holds surprises. Once you sample it, you want more.

On that theme, common faith seems to act like a superglue. Recently, at our first spiritual-renewal retreat, two participants said, "I've bonded with this group unlike any other, and I'd like to see if we could have a reunion." Our first Halftime

Fellows cohort self-organized their own reunion. A genuine circle of wounded healers is a thing of great value.

Lists are only lists, but I close this section on friendships and peers with a short list on why we need groups that regularly meet and go below the surface. From my own experience, I'm describing a Halftime group.

1. **We need to hear what other people say.** As diverse as other people's experiences and perspectives are, the take-away is that we're all human. No superheroes.

2. **We need chances to be open.** Vulnerability opens you to community, and it's a learned quality. In a group you can take reasonable chances, make mistakes, learn all the things you can't control, and reap benefits.

3. **We need to hear ourselves.** To say my thoughts out loud instead of just looping through my head is almost to hear them for the first time.

4. **We need honest pushback, both ways.** This goes back to why Jeff says Tiger Woods screwed up and lost his marriage. We need a friend who can say, "What's up with that?" Especially for high-level leaders, unvarnished honesty is at a premium.

5. **We need accountability.** We break vows to ourselves that we wouldn't break to another person. Enough said.

6. **The health benefit.** I've heard it said that 75 percent of psychotherapy goes on between friends, and I believe it. It's physically, spiritually, and psychologically helpful to have a release valve. Just google "hearts," "cholesterol," and "stress": bottling up your tension is a recipe for bad health.

You Want a Personal Board of Directors

The first time I heard Bob Buford mention a personal board of directors, I thought to myself, "I've got that." He was talking about a panel of trusted family, friends, and colleagues—people to speak truth into our lives. My board was informal, but I'd long had go-to people for wisdom, commentary, and, as needed, unwanted honesty.

Lisa, always, is my first go-to. After that, I talk with Paul Wilson, whose friendship first rewired my life. More people came to mind in specific categories. On relationship issues, Paul is my first stop. If it's about my son or daughter, I ring up a former youth leader and a good friend. For anything to do with my work/ministry, it's my Halftime coach, also a dear friend. Another good friend escorted me open-eyed into the realities of not-for-profit work. Every person, at the time, is the expert for the moment. Through the years and the circumstances, some "members" have rotated on or off the board. People form their own boards their own ways. The point is that it's foolhardy to go it alone, and I've long known that.

Because Halftime works with men and women in flux, we stress the importance of sound input. In the way public companies require an independent panel to ensure they act in the best interests of their shareholders, Halftimers need a board to act in their own best interests, to stay on mission—and to serve God and the people he tells us to love.

What can make the personal board conversation difficult, I think, is that it can take so many shapes. Just keep in mind that some form of counsel and accountability is reasonable and wise and essential. And it's hardly new. King Arthur had a round table. Franklin Roosevelt had a kitchen cabinet. It's how brain trusts and think tanks form. William Wilberforce called his personal board of directors his "chummery." Fueled by their regular meetings, Wilberforce transformed British society away from slavery. (Try taking on the United Kingdom solo.)

Proverbs 15:22 says plans fail for lack of counsel but with many counselors they succeed, and I've had a front-row seat to seeing Bob Buford live out those words. Regularly he has turned to respected and trusted counsel to help him "think my confusion out loud," and when they talk he absorbs. He often says the three top influences in his life, even though Peter died ten years ago, remain, "God—as I know him through Christ and the Scripture, and through the voice of the Holy Spirit—my wife, and Peter Drucker, whom I knew the last twenty-five years of his life."

In the second half of the twenty-first century, I can't imagine an American or Japanese marketplace leader unaware of Peter Drucker or unaffected by his teaching. Peter was the genius who made business management a discipline and forever changed how corporations give and get the best from their workers. One day when Bob was in his forties, he picked up the phone and cold-called *the* Peter Drucker, the consultant associated with America's pinnacle corporations—GM, Microsoft, and others. Bob asked Peter to advise him personally, because that was Bob. After several once-a-year meetings with Peter, Bob's only son, Ross, died tragically. When that happened, this time Peter called Bob and a deep personal bond formed. Besides changing both men, the friendship would change how America does church—a whole other story. And I urge you to read Bob's book, *Drucker & Me*.

Bob saw a source of wisdom and went after it—the "pearl of great price." Besides his God/Linda/Peter board, he formed

Bob, Inc., a regular meeting of close advisors to help him make the most of his years as circumstances changed. He'd say, "I don't see how people live without those kind of outside sources to tell you what you don't know, or what you're blind to, what's hidden in plain sight."

Maybe you're thinking: "I see wisdom in having advisors, but isn't it self-important to form a board centered around me?" Yes, if it's about you only. No, if it stands to affect your family and exponentially more lives as you work out your mission to serve. Keep in mind, too, that your board extends from friendship. My "members" genuinely want to help me be my best. And it's hardly one way. I love and care about them. I would do anything for them, and they know it.

Since we've established that your board may be formal or informal, meet frequently or as needed, be as small as three people or as large as seven (I wouldn't go larger), consider a few more criteria.

1. **Make your first and second directors your spouse and your coach.**

2. **After that, set your own parameters.** I suggest a few people in a range of ages, who are spiritually mature, are able to know your worst and want your best, are committed to your well-being, have time to invest in you, and are knowledgeable in areas that apply to your life.

3. **List your candidates and pray about them.** Person by person. Name by name.

4. **Approach them with the idea.** Describe your Halftime journey and explain why you're looking for familiar faces,

objective input, and accountability. Describe the kinds of topics or issues they may weigh in on. ("This offer would uproot my family, and my parents are disabled and need help." "What this NGO can pay won't cover college expenses." "I've never seen myself doing this, do you?") If the person shows interest, ask him or her to pray about it and agree to a one-year test drive.

5. **Set up an initial group conversation, and include your coach.** Here's where guidelines can bend. Some boards meet as groups; some are one-on-one phone conversations. My advice is to see what works and adjust until you know what's best. Keep in mind that in six months you'll have a better sense of both people and potential. If you do get together as a group, make it fun as well.

6. **Set beginning parameters.** Subject to change, you'll want to establish:

    a. Frequency (weekly, monthly, quarterly)

    b. Format (in person, phone, video chat, conference call)

    c. One-on-one or group discussions

    d. Travel (if needed) and who covers costs

    e. A balance between efficient focus on the issues and chatter/fun

Some boards exist as long as the Halftimer is in flux. Others—and the relationships in them—extend into other life decisions. Lloyd Reeb is in his fifties. As he anticipates his next decade, his board has told him to find more Lloyd Reebs—men and women to carry on what he's learned to do. He'll serve more as sage and mentor. This counsel started with his going to his board with, "What do you think?"

Of course you could hire an expert. But the difference between an expert's time and a personal board of directors is love. Impersonal "experts" (as opposed to coaches) see you from the outside and think of you, necessarily, as a commodity. A personal board member knows your inner workings and challenges and family dynamics. He or she has known you through the years. That's why transparency is the do-or-die factor. Please underline that last sentence. Someone on the outside, an expert, can say you'd be fantastic as executive pastor at a church. A friend who knows the church and knows you can say you won't fit the culture and to forget it.

At the Halftime Institute as we introduce the idea of personal boards, most people have no idea where to start, and no one they're comfortable with. No close friends. In these cases we counsel people to start small—with your spouse and coach, say. If you're at the friendship-building stage, find a group you can feel good in, and give it time. Think Bible study, a Halftime cohort, a YPO group, Pinnacle Forum. Convene. C12. 4Word for Women, an exceptional organization for professional women, was founded and headed by Halftimer Diane Paddison. You're a type A, so ask around. The groups are out there.

Halftimer Mike Samp came from a major manufacturing company where he'd been a senior exec. When work changed dramatically, he sought out the Halftime Institute and built a personal board. Halftime gave him the building blocks to discover his second half, and his group walked with him. His coach helped him flesh out the plan. But his personal board was his ongoing, sometimes daily, source of wisdom and accountability.

In Mike's second half he built a fascinating portfolio of roles around his emerging mission statement. He used his new company, Second Half Servants LLC, to equip servant leaders globally. At some point he copied Lloyd on an email he'd written about his personal board of directors:

> This group has proven to be a God-given resource of wisdom, strength and encouragement to me these past six months. I selected my wife, Lori, my senior pastor, our two financial advisers and two close Christian friends. Obviously Lori knows me best and is walking this journey with me as my partner. My senior pastor is my closest spiritual advisor. Our financial advisers have helped me re-plan our financial future. The two guy friends I asked are men of deep Christian faith. One is a long-time friend who retired from my same company 10 years ago. He is a "Paul" in my life. The other is a relatively new friend I made. He owns his own business and we were drawn together because of a mutual need for a loving but courageous brother. He is the "Barnabas" in my life. We never have board meetings (way too corporate) but they all agreed to this role and to be available whenever needed.

Halftime is the journey of your life. As they say on television: do not attempt it alone.

12

Pursue Solitude with God

In my often-halting walk with God, one sure step has been the times I've done nothing. I lob out the word "nothing" for effect, obviously, because to the untrained eye or to the overworked executive, solitude looks a whole lot like wasting time. To *doers* it can feel like a sentencing. For this recovering doer, it has been the secret to knowing and hearing from God, and it bears mentioning that Jesus set the example.

Growing up, I had an appetite to know God and no sense of how to do it, for which I don't blame the church, given my tendencies to buck every system. In my late teens I sampled God from a pocket New Testament in a cheap green cover— some departing gift as I left high school. In college that Bible stayed on my nightstand and I'd read from it.

When I finally encountered God, straight on and for myself, interestingly, it came through a friendship with Paul Wilson, underscoring again why I value relationships. One picture in my mind is Philip and the Ethiopian in that small scene in the book of Acts (8:26–40). The Ethiopian is a court official in his chariot reading the book of Isaiah. Philip asks him, "Do you understand what you're reading?" And the Ethiopian says, "How can I unless someone guides me?"

"How can I unless someone guides me?" is the relationship call to action. My guidance comes from my wife, in church, in courses and retreats, with my personal board of directors, and with my coach, Jeff. I also listen to messages from pastors whose sermons speak to me, and I take in worship music because it feeds me. Sometimes on my own I'll drill down into certain aspects of the Bible, an issue or God's character.

And yet for all that—the key relationships, church, worship, study, and so on—in my walk with God, the game changer has been stillness. Solitude. And as rewarding as it is, as profoundly as it affects my understanding and love, it remains a discipline. Like every discipline, to neglect it "just this once" for something more urgent can easily slide into skipping it altogether.

It started for me sometime after I became a Christian, in 1995, right after I was made a lay pastor at Willow Creek Community Church. As a new lay pastor, one of my first assignments, part of a group retreat, was to find a quiet place for eight hours of solitude. Hearing it, my first thought was, "You have got to be kidding. Eight hours by a stream or a tree and I'll pull my hair out." No one spoke up, however, including me, and as my group of new lay pastors fanned out, I figured my best move was to lean against a tree and open my Bible. As a reminder to my readers, my focus at the time was owning cars, boats, an airplane . . . building my net worth. That day at the tree by the stream, my Bible opened to Ecclesiastes, by King Solomon, at the time the world's wealthiest man—no small thing. Money, property, women, power; you name it and he could claim it.

Yet, "meaningless, meaningless, everything is meaningless," he wrote in Ecclesiastes:

> What do people gain from all their labors
>   at which they toil under the sun?
> Generations come and generations go,
>   but the earth remains forever.
> The sun rises and the sun sets,
>   and hurries back to where it rises.
> The wind blows to the south
>   and turns to the north;
> round and round it goes,
>   ever returning on its course.
> All streams flow into the sea,
>   yet the sea is never full.
>
>   1:3–7

Was God talking to me in this solitude?

Ecclesiastes was like reading a hybrid of *Lifestyles of the Rich and Famous* and *The Economist*. And parts of the book of Proverbs. "I undertook great projects," Solomon wrote:

> I built houses for myself and planted vineyards. I made gardens and parks and planted all kinds of fruit trees in them. . . . I bought male and female slaves and had other slaves who were born in my house. I also owned more herds and flocks than anyone in Jerusalem before me. I amassed silver and gold for myself, and the treasures of kings and provinces. I acquired male and female singers, and a harem as well—the delights of a man's heart. I became greater by far than anyone in Jerusalem before me. In all this my wisdom stayed with me.
>
> I denied myself nothing my eyes desired;
>   I refused my heart no pleasure.

My heart took delight in all my labor,
    and this was the reward for all my toil.
Yet when I surveyed all that my hands had done
    and what I had toiled to achieve,
everything was meaningless, a chasing after the wind;
    nothing was gained under the sun.

2:4–11

The Bible also says, "Come near to God and he will come near to you" (James 4:8). And here I was. And here God was.

This was my turning point. The man who had everything a person could own—and wisdom—called it meaningless, chasing after the wind. What I did for the remaining seven and a half hours, I can't say. I only know that on that day I lost my skepticism about solitude.

Back at home I began to carve out Tuesdays and Thursdays at 5 a.m., the silent hours, to take to my chair, soak in the quiet, and write in my journal. Since then I've kept some kind of weekly routine, adding a full day of solitude at least once a quarter—sometimes at home, sometimes in nature, most recently on a pontoon boat in the middle of a lake.

It's never gotten easy, and it's never failed to reward me, either at the time or later.

Many believers use solitude to read. At times I may too. Most often, though, I try to eliminate every distraction and listen only. No reading. Not even prayer. Just the space to listen for God and put on paper what comes to mind. It's that simple, that uncomplicated. Over and over, people who experience those moments or hours, even for the first time, agree that it's the most important time they spend.

As for journaling, what is it about seeing words on paper—somewhere permanent, somewhere besides in my own head?

If I struggle with worry that day, I jot down, "Lord, I'm worried," and because it's on paper I can mentally step back for perspective. "Worry . . ." I muse, and God's thoughts work into my thoughts. "Can any one of you by worrying add a single hour to your life?" (Matt. 6:27).

It's common to fear solitude, by the way; that moment when laptops close, music dies, television is off (that button should still work), and the cell phone is—brace yourself—out of commission. *Who am I*, I think, *if I'm not doing?* Answer: I am his. This thing called quiet—like every exercise or discipline or life-giving habit—is as difficult on the front end as it is rewarding in consistency.

As you read this, if the idea of sustained silence seems daunting, start with fifteen minutes. Or ten. Solitude with God is hardly punishment, but it is new, and right now it's against your nature. Remember that this is not active prayer. It's active listening. Have a pen and sheet of paper ready, or a blank book. Sit quietly and look ahead or close your eyes. Breathe easily. As thoughts enter your mind, resistance can be a form of distraction. Gently push your to-do thoughts aside, and when they return, do it again. And again. It may help to jot them down to address later. As you settle in, journal what comes to mind, no matter how crazy the thought. Later, as you consider what you wrote, share it with a trusted advisor—a coach, maybe, or someone on your personal board of directors. See what comes of it.

Early on in my pursuit of solitude, it came to me in several different ways to stop worrying about my finances. God had them under control. But what did that mean? Delete Quicken from my apps and coast on feelings? In my inexperience, I knew I needed maturity, someone acquainted both with God and with me. I was the Ethiopian needing a Philip to help me distinguish divine encouragement from my own wish fulfillment.

As I think about this now, about my love for something that once scared me, I am glancing through my journal. One entry says: "All my planning and evaluating is meaningless because at the end of the day the Lord has it figured out already, and my plans usually change." This is hardly saying not to plan. Plans matter. What it shows, I think, is my growing grip on who holds the outcome. It also hints at growing surrender. At the time, Lisa and I were looking at Liberty High School for our son, Caden, and Pepperdine for our daughter, Kennedy. I wrote, "God is in what you know is right. Let the money fall where it does."

Another time I wrote: "When Jesus tells us to die to ourselves I believe he's saying we are to enter into full surrender to him so he's fully free to guide our lives into the perfect will of God the father."

Recently in a conversation about solitude, a woman asked me: "What if I fall asleep?" Answer: sleep well. In my times with God I've been known, for up to an hour even, to drift off in his tenderness. During Halftime we see people step away for solitude and begin to nod. It's telling, and God knows what it's saying. I have a growing theory about God's connecting, reenergizing tonic of sleep. How many times do I wake up with some song in my head?

God tells us his mercies are new every morning. I think of solitude as waking rest. In ways I can never explain, in sleep and in solitude, the Lord refuels us for another day in a messy and difficult world.

"What about boredom?" the same woman asked, and she speaks for many—especially for twenty-first-century types unable to walk in nature without an iPhone and earbuds. My advice is to start with small units of time and build. In even an hour of solitude, I chalk up at least the first twenty minutes to surface thoughts before I can relax and focus. Again, too much effort fighting distractions is distracting. As errant ideas show up, maybe return to a simple phrase such as *Come, Lord Jesus* or *Be still and know that I am God.*

It's worth the time and trouble, and the fighting boredom, and falling asleep, and the false starts and the early not knowing. Freedom is discipline. Though I spend my days in a Christian nonprofit role, I fall prey to the busyness and self-importance that bind the Holy Spirit in my life. In the marketplace and world, which mostly deny God's presence, we can't sleepwalk and hope he enters into our souls. So we start toward him and he runs out to us.

Obviously I am a layperson, a pilgrim. Better believers and real theologians have written profoundly on prayer and solitude and the spiritual disciplines. Your journey through Halftime and your walk with God will fold in the wisdom of books besides this one. My point is to tell my fellow doers that intimacy with God, as with others, is essential, and that it may require doing nothing, which is mostly against our nature.

On this subject author Eugene Peterson, in a 2003 interview with Howard Butt's *The High Calling*, rang simple and true. "We're in a hurry and not used to listening," Peterson said. "We're trained to use our minds to get information and complete assignments; but the God revealed to us in Jesus and our Scriptures is infinitely personal and relational. Unless we take the time to be quiet in a listening way, in the presence of God, we never get to know him."[1]

God speaks to us? *Really?* It's easy to approach solitude thinking, "Why do other people hear you and I don't?" Looking back through journals from years ago I can see that he actually was speaking. I had to learn his voice. It's ironic how those journal entries make sense years later when they didn't at the time.

"We're not good at this. We have no practice doing it," Peterson said. "No wonder we only hear our own thoughts. This is why the church is so insistent that we [seek solitude] whether anything happens or not. Supported by 2,000 years of history, we know that God does commune with us in our listening. But because we're so unused to this way of communion, we don't hear it. So it takes time."[2]

Life gives us few one-offs. Most of the best things—marriage, health, hobbies, friendships, learning—reward us not in single moments but through time and through consistency. "God is wanting to draw us into a relationship of faith, intimacy, and love. That doesn't come through information alone," Peterson said. "It comes through trust, obedience, and the willingness to be present in the mystery of God. It comes through letting him reveal himself to us as we're able to receive the revelation. If God just dumped all the answers on us at once, we probably couldn't handle it. We'd misuse it. We'd think we had control of it now."[3]

Ecclesiastes is about the emptiness of ambition, but God appeals to ambition in one highly positive sense: he urges us to store up treasures in heaven, which never fade. In worship, relationships, reading, study, and in listening closely for his voice, I acquire the tools to add to the treasures that, unlike the ones King Solomon amassed, one day will mean everything.

13

Research, Network, and Conduct Low-Cost Probes

You paved the path. You drilled to specifics about your interests, gifts, and skills. You set a mission statement and backstopped yourself with the right people. You're learning to listen for God's voice. Now you want to research, network, and see what you like, what works. You want to begin low-cost probes. And if any part of that sounds daunting, relax and read on. It's just getting good.

In an official Halftime program, a lot of research comes from the coach, who also suggests low-cost probes and networking opportunities in your target areas. In a private Halftime group similar concepts apply, with a little more DIY (do it yourself). No matter where you end up—in your current work, in a variation of your career, or in a new field—everything in this network-and-test phase, no matter how random, will serve you. Think of a funnel. In the wide opening you pour in ideas, names, research, information, services, nonprofits, outreaches, and experiences that may align with your design. Out the narrow end comes work right for you.

Networking

About now, you're thinking: what if I'm still unsure what areas align with my passions? Start with Google. Maybe you feel strongly about children with physical disabilities. Type in "ministries for children with physical disabilities in [your city]." Doing that search for Dallas surfaces 190,000 results. It's a start.

If you use social media, employ it to announce your research: *"Facebook friends: I'm gathering basic info about local outreaches to disabled children. I'd like to talk to leaders in the field. What do you know?"* (Yes, you'll also get incidental information, and this is when you start a spreadsheet to organize even the small data coming in.)

By phone, in person, online, and through friends, spread word across church, Bible study, club, healthcare waiting rooms, and alumni organizations; in kitchen conversations; at estates sales; on the golf course; and in group and friend networks. On this mission, nobody is nobody. Tell your neighbors and your kids' friends. Never limit potential sources, and stay alert to informal clues. The truth is, you *never know*. And I have an illustration.

An attorney in Kentucky retired from the law and *labored* to involve herself with young adults through her huge church with its yards-long list of options. And nothing clicked. She and her husband, as it happens, are University of Louisville fans. Walking into a basketball game, she saw a poster about helping international students integrate into the area. It's not a "ministry" per se, but she was intrigued enough to make a phone call, and to meet with a representative of the group for lunch. Then she reasoned that she could try one dinner. Before long she was inviting foreign students to dinners (plural), making young friends, sharing her life, and, quite naturally, sharing her beliefs.

In my mind, the moral of this woman's story is that she was open and creative, willing to follow a hunch. She didn't commit a year to an organization. She picked up a phone and asked questions. Five minutes. Then a ninety-minute lunch, and she volunteered. At some point if it's God's will and doors keep opening, a person just keeps doing the next thing.

One more thought. This woman was willing to break a paradigm. She tried the youth programs at her church, and when those didn't work, she was willing to broaden to college kids at a university.

As you acquire leads on your search, remember the low cost and potentially high impact of mere follow-up. Even a twenty-minute meeting, which is easy to request, collects intel. You meet and ask: "What is a day in the life in your organization? What is your organizational model? Whom do you serve and how do these people find you? Who are your volunteers and what do they do? What are your big challenges? How are you funded and staffed? What is your budget and where is the squeeze? What are your goals and your wish list? What do you consider your 'competition'?"

If you feel a connection, you ask to volunteer for a set time, allowing for a no-fault exit. You tell your contact at the organization what you do well and the best way to use you. If you're feeling no magic, you emphasize that you are information-gathering. In every case you ask what other people you should talk to.

Either way, shortly after you interview, you handwrite a thank-you note. Right after that you record impressions on your spreadsheet. What roused your interest? What was a turnoff? What did you learn about hours, staffing, operations model, leadership, possibilities, and more?

Repeat this educational outing a few times and before you know it you've networked the local landscape of ministries to children. You've observed how different organizations operate. If you still haven't scratched your itch, refine the angle (google "disabled minority teens") and repeat. The point, as Babe Ruth—the king of both home runs and strikeouts—might say, is to keep swinging. Remember Ray in an earlier chapter who got off dead center by making sandwiches for the homeless, by just doing *something*. Anything that gets you out has potential and power. You connect with the need and observe your responses. You experience the compassion field firsthand.

Low-Cost Probes

In the mind of a Halftimer—a type A—the unspoken pressure of a low-cost probe is to make one right decision for good. Yet on the entire North American continent, no one I know has married without dating, so go easy on the expectations. The biggest mistake a Halftimer can make is to dive into major life change without testing the waters. We call that a "high-risk" probe—where a win is a bingo, but a fail pours gasoline on high-stakes consequences and then lights a match.

Low-cost probes lower your risk in three dimensions: time, money, and emotional energy—and not just for you, the Halftimer, but for your entire family. A low-cost probe is a toe in the water, and in most cases failure is a graduate-level education.

In my case I knew I wanted to serve, and I had no idea how. Before Halftime, if Bill Hybels had told me to serve in the flower-planting patrol, I would have showed up with a spade. After Halftime and a structured season of knowing myself and how God has wired me, when Willow Creek presented an opening as executive pastor/director of volunteerism and fund development, I could give an informed "no thank you."

Jeff tells a great story about a guy I'll call Randy, owner of a light manufacturing business. After a rough stretch in his life, Randy came to Christ through the Alpha Course, a twelve-week program on the Christian faith. He said to himself, "This is what I want to do," and he researched and tracked down the US Alpha director, and they met. As they met and talked, Randy realized that what had touched him was less about the Alpha syllabus than the men in his St. Louis course. They'd come around to love and care for him. That narrowed his thinking, and he began then to research every men's ministry organization in the United States. When he found the one to partner with, he reasoned, he'd sell his company and throw in with it.

And then, as if by movement-sensor, another light turned on. "One guy who works for me wears a probation ankle bracelet," he said to his coach in an enthusiastic call at 3:00 a.m. "Another guy is an alcoholic. Another's wife just kicked him out for cheating. I've got enough men's ministry right here to keep me busy for a long time."

Randy's research on men's ministry had been a study of his own heart. I can't say it too often: the journey's the thing.

During my own journey I was a lay pastor at church. Around that time I went on missions trips to Africa. I worked with special-needs kids and in a homeless shelter. And though I ended up at Halftime, every experience added to my education.

One important lesson in my education was the Sigmoid curve, which business students learn about in the life cycle of a product. It also applies to your next stage of life. In any new venture, inevitably, the line on the chart trends down before it goes up. Think about your first job out of college. I spent my first six months trying to figure out where the bathroom was and how to do the stockbroker thing. Learning curves are the down dip before skill lifts your line up and to the right. Pretty soon, if you engage and it's your calling, the line shows the trend. You flourish.

In a low-cost probe, if it's not a fit, the challenges and struggles in that early dip tell us about your gifts, skills, and passions. My early months at Halftime definitely fit the Sigmoid curve: the adjustment was a dip. But I was where I belonged, I knew about the curve, and I knew I was to stay with it.

The alternative is to grow enamored with a mission and ministry, close shop on your current work, move your family, shutter your accounts, and then fail to jell with the folks in the mission. It happens. We see people unduly admire the leader and misread (idealize) the culture they're exploring, and buy in too soon. Result: failed high-cost probe. For corporate executives, especially those dependent on in-person time, it may be hard to get away from work at all. Jeff, who stays on the front lines, had a Halftimer say, "If I tell my CEO I'm taking Thursday afternoons to find myself, he'll say, 'Hey, pal, there's twenty guys nipping at your heels. You're eighty hours or nothing.'" This guy leveraged his family vacation to be half standard American getaway, half mission trip. Together, the entire family worked in some horrible situations in other parts of the world. So touched were they that Mr. Corporate cashed in other vacation days to explore more ministries—jumping on phones before he jumped on planes. He grew confident about the time away as the family's interest grew. Doors continued to open, and at some point he was comfortable taking the time. Ultimately he pulled the ripcord, left the corporation, and joined a ministry. By then he knew what he was doing.

The average college student changes majors four times. The average Halftimer tries four low-cost probes before settling into a right Sigmoid curve. Create low-cost probes for every new season you enter, and give yourself time to fall and rise. You're dating; it's a test drive, a trial period. And if it doesn't work, file it under important lessons.

A Halftime coach will tell you that a low-cost probe may be a ten-degree course correction that would create a ministry platform at your current job. Remember the exec who stayed with Lowe's to serve the homeless in his own ranks? Think of Scott Boyer who used his business skills and pharmaceutical industry knowledge to begin to get medicine to the ROW— rest of the world.

Unless you're strongly led otherwise, start with opportunities to serve through your current work. In my case, I tried reaching out to people of other faiths and looking for ways to support people in the office. We held a Bible study off site. And I concluded that my work gained no traction. None of these probes would be long-term assignments. Yet they were incredibly valuable—and if I hadn't tried them I would still be wishing I had.

14

The Hardest Job
You'll Ever Love

Sixty percent of the men and women who complete Halftime—who have carved margin into their days; become students of their strengths, gifts, and passions; developed a concise and specific mission statement; stayed in the journey with their peers and coach; built an ongoing personal board of directors; and conducted low-cost probes—will stay in their existing careers with a new mind for mission. What was once office space is now holy ground.

This chapter is for the other 40 percent.

As Dick Anderson, at the time director of operations at Willow Creek, said to me when I complained about the finance industry (and was idealizing his "Christian" work): "If you think it's some cushy world where people are running around with halos, holding hands and singing Kumbaya, you're sadly mistaken."

Nonprofit and ministry work, for those called to it, *is* a high call—as is marketplace work. But as I've confirmed first-hand since that memorable chat with Dick, you don't want to enter nonprofit work with rosy notions. One, the work is not soft, cushy, or easy. Two, it's riddled with human nature. And three, the nonprofit world runs on rules that sometimes oppose everything you learned in the marketplace.

As a marketplace leader stepping into a nonprofit, not only do you give up your deep bench of talent but the people you bring onto your team will realize, as you will, that market-place luxuries now belong to the past. Good-bye to handing off responsibilities. Good-bye, ample budgets, plush expense accounts, easy resources, and profit. Hello again to basic tasks like writing job descriptions, which you naively thought you'd handed off years ago.

If you land among the 40 percent of Halftimers who leave corporate careers for nonprofit or ministry work, from my years at Halftime, may I salute you with a few essential eye-openers about the hardest work you'll ever love?

1. **Your standards are higher now, or should be.** When your work incentive rises, so do the stakes. In your nonprofit role, with a new sense of significance comes a new sense of responsibility. In the past you worked for owners, investors, or clients. Your shareholders were flesh and blood. Now your work has God's name somewhere on the webpage, if not in the title. The steepest expectations will be the ones you put on yourself.

2. **Discipline is more delicate.** On one hand you're more driven than ever. On the other hand, people expect a Christian organization to somehow be chill, more

forgiving. Easier. Between what you promise your do-
nors and what you ask of your staff are issues of your
leadership of others and God's leadership of you. It can
be a productive tension.

In the ministry world you'll find that some workers
resist or even resent discipline or reviews, challenges or
rebukes. "Aren't we all Christians?" the reasoning goes.
"We're supposed to support and encourage one another."
Meanwhile, you want your people happy, and this leads
into the topic of not having a deep bench.

3. **Your deep bench is gone.** The Jim Collins model is to
get the right people on the bus and then figure out where
they fit. In a nonprofit that maxim is even more important. At the same time, good talent is hard to find. Before
you hire and recruit, therefore, have a job description
and expectations, and use them.

As you build your nonprofit team, you'll meet people
eager to serve in almost any way. That's the good news.
And that's the bad news. When you post for an opening, for example, it's not a clear case of matching skills
to opportunity. Driven by their hearts, people want to
do *something.* You'll interview startlingly talented people
whose skill sets defy what you're hiring for. You'll like
these people, and the not-right-for-us conversation will
hurt. ("I'm here to serve and you're turning me away?")
But a heart to serve cannot guarantee a skill that fits.
When you wedge a great person into a "kind of right"
slot, burnout is quick.

As I was interviewed for my current Halftime role, I
must have been asked twenty times, "Do you feel called

to this role?" At some point, exasperated, I said, "No sign appeared in my front yard saying 'Dean, go work for Halftime.' I *think* this is the right role. I feel I'm being called. But I don't know for sure." Now I get it.

I walked into Halftime expecting the setup I had as managing director at Wells Fargo Advisors. But my new world had limited resources. My new team had incredible heart but people were operating outside their gifts and callings. I remember thinking, "Here's my thing. I love making sense out of chaos."

4. **Free help is never free.** No matter how it looks, there is no free help. Know the nondollar costs that come with every person in your organization. When employees raise their own support, it's tempting to move in someone more effective and just keep the first person around. But you'll pay for it. Whether it's a volunteer or someone raising support, cost happens and you need to understand how.

5. **Instead of resources, you get resourceful.** When an interviewee for a Halftime position asks me about money, if he belabors the point or tries too hard to negotiate, there's a red flag. The Halftime ministry pays a fair salary for a nonprofit but we're all in it for nontraditional compensation.

Along those lines, if you're used to having a specialist just an office or a phone call away, time to get creative—and to dust off skills from your past, like writing job descriptions and cleaning tables. Yesterday in talking to our CFO about a support person, I said, "Doesn't she have time to do that?" The answer was, "You're the boss. You're supposed to know what's going on with each of your employees." In the old days answers about a support-staff person came from that person's manager. The intermediaries are gone.

6. **You'll face some extreme expectations.** Most people think ministry should be free. At best payment is voluntary. When I arrived at Halftime, to continue to serve, the organization needed a revenue model, which made everyone incredibly uncomfortable. Make everything free, however, and the only option is to raise our budget.

   In Hong Kong a man told us we were stalling the Halftime movement by charging for it. I said, "Unless we charge, there is no Halftime movement." It's true.

7. **If you're not making money, you're asking for it.** In the marketplace you can throw money at a problem, at a proposal, or at a person you want to keep. In the nonprofit world that well is shallow, so you have to steward every resource.

8. **The rewards system changes.** You came to nonprofit work because you're no longer motivated by money. Neither are your workers, and that changes a lot of workplace dynamics. When employees raise their own support, for example, and you lay out a production plan, you can't expect instant buy-in. You may hear, "I don't feel God is calling me to that, you don't control my financial compensation, and I don't have to do it."

   How many marketplace leaders have arrived at nonprofits, held one meeting, and hit a wall? The old incentives—money, anger, intimidation, pressure, carrots, deadlines—are gone. "It immediately became a barrier to working well with people who had long been in the mission environment," one former CEO told me. He learned to reexamine and change his leadership tactics . . . and this leads to the next insight.

9. **Leadership shifts (opens) from power to influence.** When a leader can't affect performance through giving or withholding rewards, leadership style shifts from power to influence. When motivation is spiritual, conceptual, oriented toward lives—your employees may raise their own compensation—you learn to bring your team into decision making earlier, helping everyone understand why group goals advance individual passions.

10. **Accountability and results are different.** In the marketplace, accountability and metrics are built in and understood. You make a profit. You win the account. You top the previous numbers. In the nonprofit world—ministry in particular—as Peter Drucker famously told Bob Buford: "Your bottom line is changed lives." And that's a slipperier set of metrics. In the absence of accounting, track the anecdotes. One man I know kept what he called his "Book of Days"—a bound collection, year to year, of letters, emails, and notes from people telling him how his work, directly and indirectly, plays out in their lives.

    In your new world results can't trump people. Most nonprofits don't want to save the world at the expense of their workers and workers' families. They have a strong view of things like health of the individual and the workplace community. A leader has to balance worker happiness with donor wishes.

11. **Personalities are different; passions show differently.** You're from a world of high-performance, high-capacity

type A's passionate about what they bring to the table. In the old days you could pound the table and press your point of view. You could get loud, aggressive, pointed— and no one took it personally. You're in a population now of people who read aggression another way. Know that quiet is not acquiescence, and it can harden into resentment. If your staff can't engage with you, change your style to engage with them. As the marketers say, "Know your audience."

12. **Christians aren't always Christlike, and this includes you.** The dark truth in Christendom is that it's made up of fallen humans. Back to the holding-hands-and-Kumbaya picture: that ain't it. The sooner you understand that you're still working with real people and real organizational dynamics, the better.

My Advice to the 40 Percent

1. **Focus on patience and grace. Be willing to give and accept both.** Be patient with others and with yourself. You're less adaptable than you think. Be gentle with the people around you who haven't had your experiences or come from your business culture. Along those lines, be willing to admit mistakes and ask forgiveness. And never, never nurse a grudge.

2. **If you offend people, do it for the right reasons.** Jesus drew lines knowing people would fall on both sides. But there's a difference between people taking offense and your giving offense. On the front end, let people know you expect to make mistakes. Set an atmosphere

of forgiveness, if you can, and a license to laugh about conflict and shake it off.

3. **Prepare financially for your family.** A whole lot of professionals will leave the marketplace passionate for their new work and underprepared to live on a fraction of their previous income. As a CEO new to nonprofits, who did not go through Halftime, put it, "I'm sure of the choices I made but it would have been nice to have some training and coaching in financial planning to better position myself—about lifestyle, housing options, kids' plans." Halftime coaches counsel their clients to make financial prudence a key part of the transition.

4. **Focus on the call.** Halftime is built on the belief that God has a call for each person. Lock onto that truth in a person. Look for God's fingerprints and you'll find them. Ask for his leading and you'll get it. Serve the people who serve under you.

5. **Keep a sense of humor.**

Since I completed my Halftime journey—and now head the organization—I've entered the most rewarding and challenging season of my life. Afternoons I drive home with a sense of accomplishment and fulfillment because something I've done has affected not only the people around me but the kingdom of God, the people Jesus cares about.

This privilege is not exclusive to nonprofits. *All work is God's work.* All of us want to love the people Jesus loved. We want to see lives transformed. Lives are the bottom line, and nothing is more important.

15

What Finishers Know

Twenty years and tens of thousands of hours of coaching have taught this organization that the Halftimers who reach their goals rarely have—but work to get—the relationships and attitudes that can help them stay committed. Across a rich spectrum of men and women who have found their Ephesians 2:10 callings, let's discuss what finishers have in common.

1. **They know they need encouragement.** In a small group recently, one of our directors said, "I crave admiration from my fellow man." The rest of us nodded. Who doesn't know the crucial, central, imperative (where's my *Roget's Thesaurus*?) need for a pat on the back? Finishers know that affirmation is oxygen. Without it a person withers and dies.

My cautionary story on lack of feedback is a Halftimer who was clear on his calling but was a loner. We'd urged him to build a personal board of directors, but he put it off. In 2008, when the market crashed, he was especially hard hit, but worse, he had no human resources. No friendship backstop.

No cheering section. No one at all. He took the blow on his own. And in a period that destroyed many fortunes, this man, feeling unusually alone, took his own life.

2. **They accept change.** We resist change, first, because auto-pilot is comfortable. Second, because from our early twenties, studies say, we reason that the way we've always done it must be fine because it's the way we've always done it. People who finish well know a routine from a rut. They can, if need be, leave their comfort zones.

As usual, one ready example of what not to do is me. Typical case: my son comes home with short notice that his Friday night game, originally scheduled for three miles away at his middle school, has moved to a town thirty-two miles down I-45. That's inconvenient for Lisa and me, and my first thought is to say chuck it all and stay home. Do that, however, and the person who pays is my young baseball player. Long term, I pay for it in loss of relationship with him. So short term, we make the trek.

Lloyd Reeb tells the story of congressman Dan Coats from North Carolina, who retired and moved with his wife to a beach home. They'd just settled in when, at a critical time, he was offered an opportunity to serve in national politics. Instead of saying, "No, we've looked forward for years to this comfort and scenery, and we just got here," the Coatses heard it as a calling. They uprooted and relocated to the Midwest, trading great sunsets for greater life impact.

3. **They involve their spouses.** People who finish well keep their spouse's calling ahead of their own because no husband or wife can thrive while the other struggles. As a side benefit, the person you support is likely to support you in return. Either way, when a Halftimer attempts on his or her own to upend

the status quo, maybe even change careers, the partner chalks it up to midlife craziness and crevices in the relationship widen.

A strong finisher, no matter the marriage relationship at the time, sincerely asks his or her life partner, "What are your dreams and aspirations?" If the answer is, "I don't know," the next step is to (a) figure it out together, or (b) bring in a knowledgeable third party. At Halftime, we learned the hard way to involve spouses in our programs because unless those God put together row together, the boat goes in circles.

4. **They significantly involve others.** Friends and a peer group, a coach, a board of directors . . . however you do it, no one makes it alone. It takes outside truth to effect inner change, and finishers know to get it. The basic requirements to populate your life include humility, listening skills, and initiative. Oh, and follow-through. When you get good advice or input, you act on it.

5. **They work to get physically healthy and stay that way.** Once upon a time in America people grew up, married, and gained weight. One, two, three. Then one day in 1977, a man named James Fixx published *The Complete Book of Running*, and adult fitness came in from the fringe. People you knew—not just hardcore athletes—purchased tennis shoes and sweats and used 'em. After a while these people credited their exercise with benefits like clearer minds, lower stress, weight loss, longer life expectancy, better attitudes, even resistance to certain diseases.

Ironically, James Fixx died at age fifty-two of a heart attack— his father had died of a heart attack at age forty-three. But also note that when James began running, at age thirty-five, he smoked two packs a day and weighed 214 pounds. Fitness may or may not have lengthened his life, but I'd wager it vastly improved the years he had.

More than a few men and women, achievers with great things to give the world, have come to Halftime to finish well and, from decades of stress, hit-and-miss diets, minimal sleep, and exercise as an afterthought (if at all), died before they could start.

Clark Millspaugh was a different case. From his Halftime involvement and coaching, and in his personal moments, Clark—a fit man in his fifties—had drawn close to God and pursued his Halftime journey. He aimed his market-sharp skills at inner-city Tulsa, a food desert, where he started a school, a grocery store, a clinic, and more. Then, within just a year or two of launching several life-giving enterprises, Clark's doctor diagnosed cancer and he was gone. My point is not just about living longer but living better in the time we're given—a length of time no one can know. Our bodies are temples, and we are not our own.

Small final note: About a year ago a friend of mine suggested that I start running, which I particularly hated—but I was desperate to feel better, to fit in my clothes, to find some energy. The first time I walked outside to run, I covered less than two blocks, but the key was having someone to run with.

In the past six months I've run four half marathons and averaged twenty-five to thirty miles a week, which I credit to not running alone. So aim your problem-solving skills at your personal health. Survey the product (you), network for good outside counsel (doctors, trainers, fitness centers, jogging clubs, equipment, and ideas), set *realistic* goals, and work back to doable strategy. And of course, as in any project, your personal desire to skip a given workout is pretty much irrelevant.

6. **They keep the spiritual lines warm.** Jesus says he is the vine and we are the branches. Apart from him we can do

nothing. From personal experience, I know it's true. And so is the reverse: with him, we can do anything. People who finish well know that almost nothing that matters in life is a one-off. Just as we eat, sleep, exercise, and stay in touch with our spouse daily—so we daily connect and reconnect to the vine.

———— ◆ ————

When Bob Buford wrote about one person's journey, he started a movement. I write now from a twenty-year movement to bring it back to one person: you. Where Bob lacked data, he had determination. Determination is still necessary, but you now have the stories, relationships, successes, and failures to help you trade up for real.

If you come on the journey, read this list multiple times. Tape it to your mirror. Build the community, the perspective, the spiritual practices, and the health to put you in the best position for a strong second half.

It's what gives meaning to everything else.

He Established My Steps

He also brought me up out of a horrible pit,
Out of the miry clay,
And set my feet on a rock,
And established my steps.
He has put a new song in my mouth.

—Psalm 40:2–3 MEV

The Hiding Place is the story of Corrie ten Boom, a forty-five-year-old spinster in the Netherlands in the 1940s. As the book begins, she helps her elderly father run the family watch shop. Nazis invade the Netherlands, the ten Booms—through their business and home—save scores, maybe hundreds, of Jewish lives, and eventually, of course, are found out. Shortly after their arrest, Corrie's father dies. Later Corrie will watch bitterly as her beloved sister, Betsy, wastes away in a concentration camp.

But Betsy has said to her, and Corrie learns for herself, that "no pit is so deep that God is not deeper still." And on that high note I end *Trade Up*.

No life is so mangled, no job so empty, no marriage so battered, no decision so misguided that God is not steps ahead, ready to break ground and open a new road. His mercy is endless. His plan is not to punish or condemn but to stop the abuse you inflict on yourself. He'll use any opportunity to woo you to his peace and to your created purpose, and his ways are ingenious. We think we come to him, but all along he is coming for us.

Why wait? The worst years, the worst mistakes—however damaging or stupid or greedy—are redeemable. In my life that kind of grace shows everywhere, starting with Lisa. Tullis, my buddy through so many chapters, is now a believer, a vascular surgeon happily married to Michelle, and father of their daughter, Reagan. The redemption around me is a long list—how much time do you have?

A few nights ago, I read aloud the early chapters of this book, the ones strictly about me, to Lisa and her parents. My in-laws commented, "You were not a nice guy." And they're right. I won't hide it. The life that ping-ponged from the Midwest to the West Coast and back to the Midwest before rolling to a stop in Dallas, Texas, never deserved this goodness. From lost to found, from meeting Paul to Willow Creek and Lisa, to Bob Buford and Dallas . . . from playing the market to investing in lives, surely my story proves, as the saying goes, that there is a God and it's not me.

Trade Up is my story not just from Wausau to Dallas but from smoldering discontent to beginning to order my days so that God could order my steps.

Those steps, I'll add, hardly end with this life. There's far more than here, far more than now. Right now we see through a glass darkly. One author says that this life, for all its bruises and struggles and pain, is just a birth canal to the real life that awaits us.

And so, to borrow a closing I particularly like: *Onward.*

The *Trade Up* Study Guide

BEST PRACTICES FOR YOUR
HALFTIME JOURNEY

For serious students of the Halftime journey, *Trade Up* is purposely short, and it offers this brief study guide—a recap of best practices—from chapters 5 to 13, the instruction chapters. Short chapters and a study guide lend themselves, I hope, to airplane reading and a deep dive (you, not the plane) into the relationships and conversations that can help you get to your best second half.

Have I made it clear that it won't be easy? Is it clear that you must be intentional, that it takes work to know yourself, and that the magic comes out of authentic community?

Check, check, check?

Then I hope you'll find this study guide helpful, always in tandem with the chapters. Build and draw on every resource. Never give up. And don't be a stranger. Let me know what happens for you, in you, and around you.

Chapter 5: Start with the End in Mind

Chapter 5 is your setup, the dreams-and-vision kickoff—as in, what are your dreams and vision? If your fallback answer is to say you don't know, try one mental exercise and three pointed questions.

1. **Imagine your eightieth birthday.** You walk into your favorite restaurant and realize it's a large birthday party for you. Friends and family have gathered to recap your role in their lives. One by one, as they approach the microphone, what do you find yourself hoping they say? Write it down.

2. **Answer three questions.** On that same sheet of paper, write down and answer three all-important questions:
   a. What is all your gaining costing you?
   b. What in your life has the greatest value and how do you protect it?
   c. If you were to reorder your life to finish well, what evidence would confirm that you were on the right track?

3. **Save your work.** Keep your paper to consider your answers in depth later with a counselor, mentor, or small group.

Chapter 6: Open Your Time and Space

In chapter 6 you take specific steps to open space in your time and treasures. From my own journey, and from the Halftime notebook, this chapter includes a dazzling little chart to help you identify and weigh your activities and priorities. I also list several questions that helped me evaluate what I wanted to hold on to versus what could be holding me back.

Chapter 6 helps you:

1. **Look at your schedule and create margin in your life.**
   The essential first Halftime exercise is the great opening
   of the calendars. Read the directions in this chapter to
   build a personal spreadsheet like the graphic provided.
   List your activities and rank them as priorities. Then
   consider how to double up on some and delete others.

2. **Assess your possessions and create margin in your "treasure."** Ownership adds responsibility; excess ownership
   steals from your life's real treasures. Chapter 6 details
   my own ownership housecleaning, for better or worse,
   and offers a few questions that may help in yours:

   a. Does this thing I own take up more time than I can
      justify?

   b. Is it a financial drain?

   c. Is it a physical drain, causing anxiety and stress?

   d. Is it in any sense an idol, something that replaces God
      in my life? (Even physical fitness can become an idol
      when concern for appearance trumps concern for my
      soul.)

   e. Does it take time from my family?

   f. Do I truly want it, or by chance do I own it to impress
      myself or someone else?

Chapter 7: Know Your Strengths

"Know thyself" is neither Shakespeare nor Saint Paul. For our
purposes, it's Halftime. To know where you thrive requires
first that you know *you*. And odd as it seems, most of us don't

know ourselves. Chapter 7 goes into some detail toward remedying that. In this chapter, you:

1. **Learn your strengths.** Buy a copy of *StrengthsFinder*. Read it, and take the exam.
2. **Share the wealth of insight.** As possible, have the people around you—family members and coworkers—assess their strengths.
3. **Discuss.** When you identify your top five strengths, discuss them with your group, your spouse and family, your coworkers, your board of directors, and your coach. Outside perspectives are essential.

Chapter 8: Know Your Spiritual Gifts

Whether you're on the Halftime journey or not, if you're a Christian, you want to know your spiritual gifts and how they equip you to serve. In chapter 8 you are urged to:

1. **Do it now.** Start by calling your church or going online to take a basic inventory quiz.
2. **When you know your gifts, apply five questions.** To put your gifts in context, ask:
   a. How do they compare and contrast with my *StrengthsFinder* results?
   b. How do my spiritual gifts complement my strengths?
   c. Which gifts resonate most deeply with me in this period of my life?
   d. Which would I be most excited to leverage in my second half?

    e. How might I use all these gifts more often and more effectively?

3. **Take any questions or concerns to your pastor.** Different denominations have different takes on certain gifts. If something stirs up questions, start with your pastor.

4. **Does it give me joy?** List ten situations, large and small, in which you've used your gifts and consider how they dovetail with your strengths. Regarding each activity, did it give you joy? Why or why not? Review your list and answers with your team and your coach.

Chapter 9: Know Your Passion

Ah, passion. Even when it wanes, to know one's passion is to know it will return and direct you, like the needle on a compass. But how many people come to Halftime believing they have no passion at all? Answer: more than I ever expected. So we help them with these highly effective assignments.

1. **If you already know your passion, write it down.** If you know what cause, suffering, issue, or people group moves you—that wrong you could lose yourself in trying to right—describe it. What affects you? Why? What would you like to see happen on behalf of that group or issue?

2. **If not, ask four questions.** If you don't know your passion, take on these four questions/tasks:
    a. Of the needs across the world today—or in your house or next door—what makes you sad, glad, or angry?
    b. As you read *USA Today* for a week, what topics grab your attention and why? What makes you sad, glad, or angry? What does *not* move you?

    c. When you lose all sense of time, what are you doing?

    d. What in your life stirs feelings of shame? Where are you deeply wounded? Is it possible that your dark night of the soul could light someone else's path?

3. **Learn about what moved Jesus.** Refer in this chapter to the list of types of people Jesus loved. What, if anything, does that stir in you? In your community or surroundings, what needs, issues, or ministries apply to specific groups on this list?

4. **Get feedback.** This is important. If you believe you've heard from or been nudged by the Holy Spirit, say as much to your coach, mentor, or group. If not, say that too.

Chapter 10: State Your Mission

No corporation would march into the marketplace without a mission statement, and neither can you. It's that simple, though, as the saying goes, simple doesn't mean easy. Chapter 10 outlines practical means for you to draft and continue to refine a mission statement that becomes your filter for saying yes or no.

1. **Draft and polish your mission statement.** Working with your group and coach, in fifty words or fewer, draft a statement that identifies (1) your gifts, (2) the group you feel called to serve, and (3) your desired outcome. Expect it to take some time. Allow for multiple iterations. As word gets out that you're looking to serve, and as you begin to explore your interests and options, your mission statement—always subject to tweaking and changes—is your filter. In every case, the more specific your statement the better the filter. (The chapter has some great examples.)

If you don't know your mission statement, draw a picture. If you can't come up with a group you want to serve, walk up to a whiteboard or sit down to a blank sheet of paper. *Using no words*, pictures only, sketch your gifts, the people who pull at your heart, and what you would want for them.

And if you still don't have it, don't panic. Every part of the journey prepares you for the destination. As you read in this chapter, you can use one or all of these steps to better know what moves you to mission:

a. **Write.** Write about when you were lost in the pleasure of using your gifts. Write about something that moves you, or something you enjoy deeply. Then, preferably with a peer group or coach, review it for insights.

b. **Talk.** Go back to your peer group for ideas and input. Your coach also should have leading questions. Talk about the books you read, the shows you watch, how you spend your spare time.

c. **Read.** Return to *USA Today* articles to see what makes you glad, sad, or mad (or bored—because that tells you something, too).

d. **Look inside.** Talk with someone you trust, your group or your coach, about your greatest pain and consider what compassion that gives you for others, or if it prevents you from showing compassion.

Chapter 11: Populate Your Journey

You should be able to count on a motivational book for motivational sayings, so here's a trusty one: You alone can do it, but you don't have to do it alone. Chapter 11 spells out clear steps to get yourself into community, which your journey—and you—require. Period.

1. **Bring your spouse into the journey.** The Halftime journey to the work God has for you is a misfire until your spouse is also fulfilled in his or her dreams and aspirations. And until your spouse endorses your journey, you're not ready to launch. This chapter includes several pieces of marriage-enhancing advice:

   a. Ask your spouse a three-part question: What are your dreams for one year, three years, and ten years from now? Answer each on three levels: for you as a child of God, for us as a couple, and for us as a family. When you have the answers, go out to dinner to unwind and read through them.

2. **Build a personal board of directors.** In the way the sailors of old needed the stars, a Halftimer needs a personal board of directors for the committed (and informed) objectivity that family, friends, and colleagues can provide.

   a. **Your first two directors are your spouse and your Halftime coach.**

   b. **Set your parameters.** You want people who are spiritually mature, know you well, cover a range of ages, want your well-being, have the time, and are knowledgeable in areas that apply to you.

   c. **List your candidates and pray for them.** Person by person, name by name.

   d. **Approach them with the idea.** "What would you think about . . . ?"

e. **Set up an initial group conversation (and include your coach).** Some boards meet in person; some meetings are by phone. See what works and allow for changes until you get it right. If you do get together as a group, make it fun as well as work.

f. **Lay the ground rules.** Subject to change, you'll want to establish:

- Frequency (weekly, monthly, quarterly)
- Format (in person, phone, video chat, conference call)
- One-on-one or group discussions
- Travel (if needed) and who covers costs
- A balance between efficient focus on the issues and chatter/fun

Chapter 12: Pursue Solitude with God

1. **Start simply.** To begin to pursue solitude, set aside five to fifteen minutes. Keep handy a pen and paper. If you fall asleep, not to worry. Trust God and thank him for the rest. If you're bored, allow for it. Chalk up at least the first twenty minutes to surface thoughts. As errant ideas show up, return to a word or phrase such as *Come, Lord Jesus* or *Be still and know that I am God.*

2. **Don't overwork on distractions.** Sit quietly and look ahead or close your eyes. Breathe easily. As thoughts enter your mind, resistance can be its own distraction. Gently push all to-do thoughts aside, and when they return, gently push them aside again. And again. Maybe jot them down to address later.

3. **Journal what comes to mind.** As you settle in, no matter how crazy the thought, journal what occurs to you. Later, as you consider what you wrote, share it with a trusted advisor—a coach, maybe, or someone on your personal board of directors. See what comes of it.

4. **If you need insight, seek it.** If anything about what you've written confuses you or raises questions, talk it over with a good friend, your coach, or someone with spiritual maturity.

5. **Keep your journal to refer back.** You'll see progress in your understanding and have an ongoing record of God's love—even when you didn't see it at the time.

Chapter 13: Research, Network, and Conduct Low-Cost Probes

Until now all your work has been to build a launch pad. Now to *try out your ideas.* The only thing that can keep you from ultimate success is to fail to try. The point is to keep trying.

1. **Exercise your mission statement.** Use it to direct your research and information gathering. Your plan is to (1) talk to/interview leaders in your fields of interest, and (2) as you feel a connection, volunteer in the organization for a preset length of time. You're there to learn the landscape, and Google is your first friend. Never underestimate the power of a one-hour internet search or a five-minute phone call.

2. **Start small and grow.** To learn the landscape, start with your pastor, your friends, your personal board of directors.

"Who needs help and what kind?" you ask. And of course, you don't have to follow every lead. Go to Facebook, your husband's hunting partner, kids' friends, church groups, other clients in your doctors' waiting rooms . . . ask questions, let people know you're looking, and listen up.

3. **Build a network.** After every in-person meeting, send a handwritten thank you. After every significant email or phone call, email a thank you. The knowledge you gain and relationships you are forming will continue to serve you.

4. **Warm up the ancillary lines.** If an organization interests you, talk to a nonleader there. Sound 'em out.

5. **Record your impressions.** Establish a set of criteria about the organization, its leader, the culture, model, volunteers, and effectiveness—and build a spreadsheet to document (eventually to compare and contrast) what you learn, who you see, and what you think.

This study guide is what it is: a guide. You might even want to use it in a small group. In every case, you want to read the chapter, preferably with someone else. And in every case, you should interact deeply with the people on the journey with you and the people advising you. Keep notes. Use that spreadsheet. Gather information. Stay open. And God bless you.

Notes

Chapter 3 Marriage, Divorce, and Real Love

1. Bob Buford, *Drucker & Me* (Brentwood, TN: Worthy Publishing, 2014).

Chapter 5 Start with the End in Mind

1. Colby Itkowitz, "Harvard researchers discovered the one thing everyone needs for happier, healthier lives," *Washington Post*, March 2, 2016, https://www.washingtonpost.com/news/inspired-life/wp/2016/03/02/harvard-researchers-discovered-the-one-thing-everyone-needs-for-happier-healthier-lives/.

2. Mount Sinaï Medical Center, "Have a Sense of Purpose in Life? It May Protect Your Heart," ScienceDaily.com, March 6, 2015, https://www.sciencedaily.com/releases/2015/03/150306132538.htm.

3. "Jimmy Fallon Explains His Finger Injury," YouTube video, 7:25, from *The Tonight Show Starring Jimmy Fallon*, July 13, 2015, https://www.youtube.com/watch?v=CztT_pBFQv8.

Chapter 11 Populate Your Journey

1. C. S. Lewis, *The Four Loves* (New York: Harcourt Brace, 1960), 78.

Chapter 12 Pursue Solitude with God

1. "Interview with Eugene Peterson: Why Can't I Hear God?" *The High Calling*, undated, https://www.theologyofwork.org/the-high-calling/blog/interview-eugene-peterson-why-cant-i-hear-god (accessed 28 July 2016).

2. Ibid.

3. Ibid.

Dean Niewolny spent twenty-three years in executive roles with three of Wall Street's largest financial firms, finally as market manager for Wells Fargo Advisors in Chicago, where he oversaw a $100 million market.

In 2010, Dean traded his marketplace career for Halftime to help people who, like him, want to translate their own "first half" success and skills into affecting lives. Joining Halftime as managing director, in 2011 he became chief executive officer.

These days Dean speaks worldwide, encouraging business leaders to channel first-half achievement into a second half joy, impact, and balance. He says, "While the appetite for significance is at an all-time high, most people have no idea where or how to know their gifts and talent—and to connect to their passions. Nothing satisfies me more than to help a man or woman say, 'This is what God has for me to do.'"

Having played sports from Little League to semi-professional baseball, Dean still enjoys coaching youth sports, especially his son's Little League teams. He and Lisa have two children and live in Southlake, Texas.

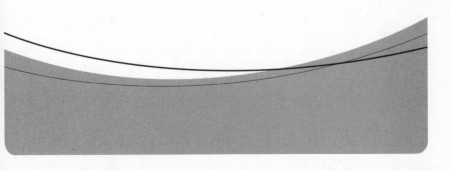